THREE

THREE

Acid, Texture, Contrast

The essential foundations to redefine everyday cooking

Selin
Kiazim

Photography by
Chris Terry

Hardie Grant

QUADRILLE

CONTENTS

4

INTRO

The idea behind *Three* is simple: to share with passionate fellow cooks the foundational tools I use on a daily basis, at home and in my restaurants, to create my dishes. My hope is that home cooks will use the three building blocks of acid, texture and contrast to turn good dishes into knockout dishes, and become more intuitive and playful cooks in the process.

I am a keen cookbook reader myself. When I say keen, I mean that there are cookbooks displayed all over the living room and kitchen, and the bookcase is the site of a perpetual jostle for space between books dedicated to food and the reading books of my partner. She wins, but barely.

She is the kind of person I had in mind when writing this cookbook. She is a foodie, and she and I have no problem sitting down and devouring a restaurant meal usually reserved for a group of three or four. Eating with her is a joy: she is adventurous, willing to try new things and push the boat out, and is slowly building a palate for dishes that work.

Having said that, she is far less shiny and accomplished than me in the kitchen (I write this with her full knowledge and permission). The basics are there – cutting, slicing, roasting, steaming – but she has yet to graduate from reading recipes step by step and not daring to veer off the straight and narrow, to being

"...use the three building blocks of acid, texture and contrast to turn good dishes into knockout dishes"

able to create simple but flavourful dishes herself without the reassurance of someone else's words. Her lack of confidence in the kitchen has baffled me, especially for such an accomplished eater.

I gradually realized that she and I, at the end of the day, speak a different language. I took for granted that the fundamentals of a professional chef's brain might not necessarily be shared with other, non-chef, people. (This should tell you a little bit about how insular and single-minded chefs' visions can sometimes be.) This cookbook is written for people like her and, as you're here reading this, people like you. I wanted to write a cookbook of creative, delicious recipes but also one full of knowledge, ideas and inspirations, to help make the leap from following recipes to the final full stop, to begin building a repertoire you can call your own.

When I think back through my professional career (and a whole lot of dishes cooked at home as well), every single one that passed the cut (ended up on the menu, or came back Sunday after Sunday) was perfectly balanced

with acidity, with interesting texture, and with a pleasing and surprising contrast. Keep these three – acid, texture, and contrast – at the forefront of your mind, and you are on the way to flavour.

And while the concept behind *Three* is simple, the effect is anything but.

Take this book as permission to experiment. Try out the recipes and feed them to family, friends, strangers. Get inspired and make a meal you never thought possible. Get your hands and your brain used to dressing a potato salad and seeing the way in which lemon and oil interact, and then make a spectacular dressing of your own. Open the kitchen cupboards on a Wednesday night, pull out three random ingredients and try your hand at making a dish you cannot stop eating, however hard you try to put your fork down. Take one of my recipes and play around with the ingredients, and pass it off as your own – because it will be yours. *Three* will give you the tools and confidence to have fun with your food.

Now, go and play…

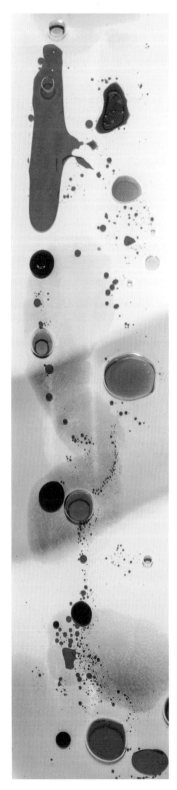

How to Use This Book

Three is, at its core, a cookbook, and you will find recipes (p.90 onwards) in the second part of this book to suit every appetite and every occasion. The chapters are divided into key ingredients, and the idea is that perhaps two to three of these recipes would come together to create a complete meal. Having said that, some can stand alone and will be a beautiful lunch or dinner, and some will work really well as part of a spread or fancy dinner party (in which case, go wild with how many you prep, and make sure to spread the work out over a couple of days, as many of these recipes will keep perfectly well). Some recipes will include alternative ideas and inspirations, and you should see these as an invitation to play around with the original and make it your own.

A small note on plating. I am, in my heart of hearts, a chef. My dishes therefore contain the odd dollop, smear, and artfully arranged bit of crunch on the top.

Rather than letting this intimidate you, I would ask you to give it a go. We eat with our eyes, and a beautifully arranged dish is sure to elicit some very satisfying 'oohs' and 'aahs' from your guests. Most importantly, good plating is not something that should just be reserved for the restaurant pass. I believe that with a little bit of practice anyone can do it. All you need is a spoon, a dollop of patience and a bit of creativity. No cheffy tweezers needed, I promise.

Alternatively, you could also just chuck it all on a plate! At the very end of the day, it's the flavour that counts.

The first part of the book, the *Know-How* section (p.10), is where you will gain your real confidence as a cook, and shouldn't be skipped.

The *Basics* section (p.12) will give you just that – the basics. It is my belief that if you get sourcing, tasting, and key ingredients such as herbs, oils, and vinegars down, you're already halfway there.

The building blocks of this book are, of course, acid, texture, and contrast, and all of the recipes in *Three* will have these at their very core. *Foundations* (p.20) goes into these in depth. Read it and let it sink in, but above all, take this knowledge and go taste, try, and create.

In *Ideas & Inspirations* (p.36), you will find short recipes – for toppings, dressings, purées and the like – to which many of my longer recipes will refer for variations upon a dish. But reading through them will open up a warren of possibilities. I fully encourage you to take what you need from them, and to use these recipes to add to your own, or to create new ones that will surprise you and your chosen eating partners in equal measure.

Key:

VG – vegan
V – vegetarian

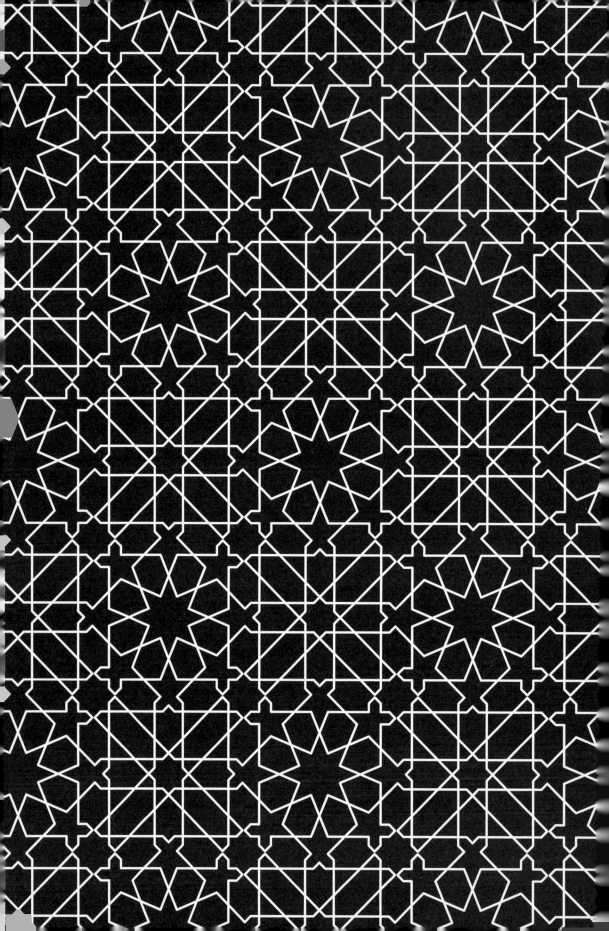

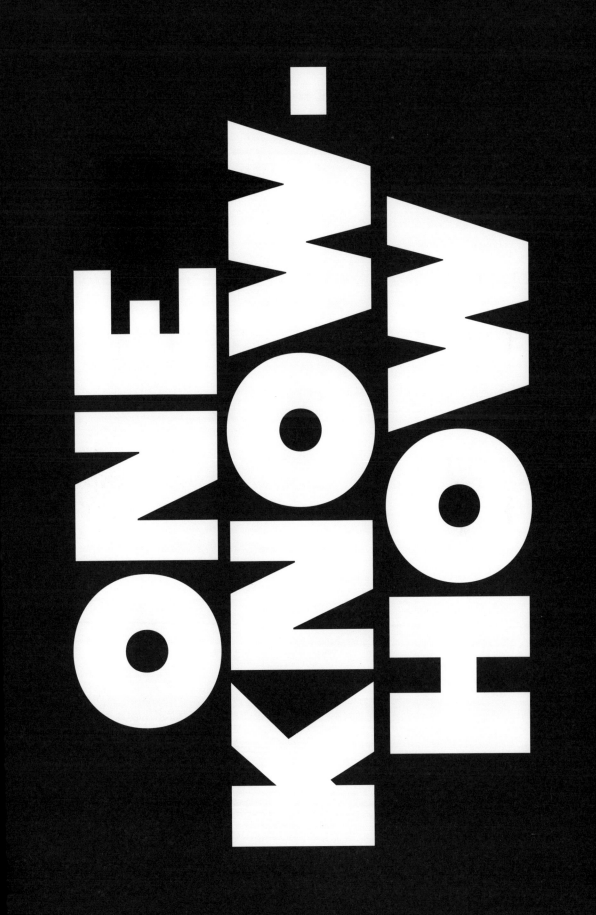

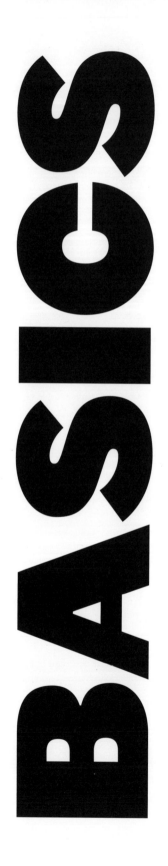

BASICS

Sourcing

We chefs bang on about quality ingredients, and for some of you, this may feel like a faraway goal or too expensive an exercise. Much has been said, but here's my tuppence-worth for the sake of the recipes in this book.

Good food isn't cheap and, as I write this in 2021, I can see prices of ingredients rise even more. The key to buying produce is to do what is within your means. That could mean visiting a farmers' market or it could mean shopping in a supermarket. Wherever you are, spend time looking at where the produce comes from. I have never understood why we should want to buy brown onions bagged in plastic and flown in from New Zealand when they grow perfectly well in UK soil. The planet really has enough to deal with without us flying our basics halfway around the world.

Local is better because fruit and veg that is picked at the height of its season, and served fresh (having spent as little time travelling as possible), is bound to taste better. I also try to avoid putting unnecessary pesticides into my body – the same goes for ingredients when I have no idea what they mean or why they are in a product – so I shop organic where I can. This isn't always possible, so an alternative to look out for is 'minimal intervention', which is what I'd expect from the bounty you'll find at farmers' markets. If you're unsure, just ask.

There is another reason, of course, for shopping small, local and independent. I'm not talking about those beautiful, artisanal and organic shops with rows of seductive (and very expensive) produce – although those are great to treat yourself or get something that is not available anywhere else. I'm talking about the corner shop, the greengrocer, and your two-woman bakery. I certainly pop into a nearby supermarket once in a while (if I need some last-minute things), but I try to spend my money on those vendors who are likely to circulate that money back into the local community.

Another great example of this is restaurant suppliers. During Covid-19, many of them turned to supplying home cooks through delivery and many have continued to do so. They are used to receiving tons of questions from us chefs, and so are usually very capable of telling you what is in season, where something was grown, and sometimes can even tell you exactly whose hands pulled that turnip out of the soil. Get in touch with your favourite local restaurants to find out who supplies them and then simply look up their websites for their delivery details.

Once you've decided where to buy your produce, touch and test it – that's my mum's influence, right there, master market-shopper and a deft hand at haggling down prices, too – and cook with as much colour as you can find. Instead of your regular green beans, try yellow and purple ones; go crazy with a rainbow of radishes in red, pink, purple, yellow, and black. Colours are a great source of contrast, and they please the eye too, which is an important part of eating. They get your mouth watering, and on top of all of that, a rainbow of fruit and veg brings a welcome variety of vitamins, minerals and antioxidants.

Protein is usually the most expensive part of a shopping list. In the past couple of years, I have made a conscious decision to eat only sustainably reared and produced fish, meat, eggs and dairy, with as little mileage between my plate and its place of birth. I eat less fish and meat so that when I do want it, I can splash out on that delicious well-reared steak from my lovely butcher's down the road. Same goes for fish. The UK has plenty of hard-working fishermen and fisherwomen plying its waters, and trust me when I say, once you have a grilled mackerel, caught less than 24 hours ago in Cornish waters, you'll never go back.

So eat less of it, but eat better, and get thrifty and creative with the meat or fish you do buy. Use bones to make broths; if you buy a leg of lamb or a pork shoulder, cut a bit off before cooking and dice it up really small, cook it with onion and potatoes and serve alongside a vibrant salad; and use your leftover roast to make a hash, to toss through noodles, or make fried rice.

Tasting

Taste everything. Taste often, taste repeatedly, taste with care. If I have spent a day in the kitchen, I will often skip dinner. I will have stuck a (clean) spoon in so many pots, pans, and roasting trays it will have filled me right up. But, it's the only way to cook: tasting is absolutely essential.

I can write you a book but, unfortunately, I cannot give you my taste buds. You might have a very refined palate already, or, like my partner often says about hers, you may feel you have none. I truly believe taste buds and palates can be trained and if you taste your cooking often enough, during various stages of the process, you will gradually build up an instinctual sense of what a dish needs. You will also start to understand your own preferences more. Personally I like my food quite acidic, quite salty, and with bags of flavour that are not afraid to smack me around the taste buds now and then. You may prefer something a bit more subtle, and you have the freedom to take my recipes and measurements as guides rather than rules, taking away and adding where you feel it is needed. This also goes for sauces and dressings; you may be someone who just likes less sauce, in which case I suggest you save any leftovers from a recipe and use it for something else later in the week. Remember, you can add a bit more but you can't take away, so it is better to start slowly when dressing rather than going all-in right away.

Tasting is not only important for judging flavour but often whether something is cooked or not. If a recipe says to cook the vegetables for 5 minutes or until soft, for example, I suggest you taste them throughout to see how they are coming along. No two vegetables are the same and it may take less or more time depending on what mood your particular vegetable is in that day. You should also always go with your instinct and preference; I may prefer things a bit charred where you would have rather stopped at golden-brown.

Trust yourself and your taste buds, whatever developmental stage they're in. Often, I feel there is an intrinsic worry in less-experienced cooks about what is 'allowed' or 'accepted' or 'tasty'. Let me tell you now: they are whatever you define them to be. Your taste buds will tell you when they don't like something and when it's not to their particular taste – whether something is too salty or too mushy or too charred – in which case, listen to them and adjust accordingly.

Herbs

Herbs are a pretty essential part of my cooking, so I think they deserve a mention here. I usually have bunches of parsley, coriander (cilantro) and perhaps a little thyme in my fridge. I like to wash them straight away. Just fill your sink with cold water and ruffle your herbs about to ensure all the soil and other unwanted bits sink to the bottom. They can then hang out in colanders, on baking racks with trays underneath, or on a clean dish towel until they are dry most of the way, if not all of the

way. Drier is better, as dressings will cling to them more readily. I like to wrap the herbs into bundles, in paper towels, and store all herbs in one box.

When you're ready to cook, just pick the leaves of tarragon, basil, mint and thyme. For coriander (cilantro) and parsley, which are probably the herbs I use most, I like to pick the leaves along with a little bit of the stem so they stand proud.

Oils

I don't have the biggest range of oils in my larder, but I do have the right oil for the right job. I can't live without extra-virgin olive oil – that much should be clear from the recipes in this book. I use it in most of my dressings and a lot of the cooking, too. There are purists out there who believe you should never cook with olive oil because it will burn and become bitter. There is some truth to this, but I come from a family of proud olive oil users and there really is no arguing with my grandmother's (olive oil) fried red mullet. Olive oil is used for cooking right across the Mediterranean and Middle East, in copious amounts.

My suggestion is to use (for cooking) a decent olive oil – by no means your most expensive one, that would be a waste – with a flavour profile that leans towards fruity and sweet rather than naturally bitter (which would be accentuated by any cooking). Olive oil does have a lower smoking temperature, but I find that it works perfectly fine. My favourite is Arbequina olive oil. I have a big blue can of it in

my house, and it is good for cooking with, as well as dousing over some anchovies or as part of a salad dressing.

I always have a bottle of sesame oil on hand – a must for recreating or evoking dishes all over Asia. You should never cook with sesame oil, however, as the smoking point is really low and it will go bitter very quickly.

For a plain oil I usually have a sunflower, vegetable or grapeseed oil knocking around. With their high smoking points and neutral flavour, these oils are particularly good for shallow and deep frying. Grapeseed is probably the most versatile of the three: it fries and cooks well, but is also suited for mayonnaises and herb oils.

Vinegars

There are a hundred and one vinegars out there, and I am not one to dictate which you should choose. You will notice I have given you a range of vinegars to work with in the recipes; the idea is that you should use whichever one you already happen to have in the store cupboard, rather than getting hung up on buying a specific one. Personally, I always have white wine, red wine, apple cider, balsamic, sherry, moscatel and rice wine vinegars in my pantry. Fancier options will pass through from time to time, like chardonnay, cabernet sauvignon or Pedro Ximenez vinegars.

If you're just beginning to build up a vinegar collection, you can't go wrong with a decent moscatel, red wine and sherry vinegar.

Salts

I use two salts in my cooking: one is a fine salt and one is flaky sea salt. For the latter, I am mildly obsessed with Maldon salt. I did an interview on the radio a couple of years ago, and I told the presenter the one thing I would take with me if I had to go and live on a deserted island was Maldon salt. I reckon the team at Maldon got a bit excited over this, and the salt pig – their signature earthenware salt jar – they sent me in the post has moved with me from house to house ever since. I personally finish almost all of my dishes with a few sprinkles of sea salt, right at the very end before serving: at this point, it's no longer about seasoning but rather about the flavour-on-steroids effect of those flakes popping off in your mouth.

For fine salt I would recommend getting as pure a product as possible. Don't go for something that says 'table salt' as this is the highly refined stuff (and often contains ingredients that have no place being there); instead, look for a finely ground sea salt.

FOUND-ATIONS

I spent my younger years in North London where, every Sunday like clockwork, the skies would fill up with the smoke and aromas of dozens of Turkish-Cypriot and Greek-Cypriot barbecues (or 'mangals', in Turkish) being lit at the same time. No barbecue was complete without the simple tomato, onion and parsley salad, dressed with lemon juice and salt, to accompany piles of grilled meats. The acidity mixed with strong onion pungency was perfect to cut through all of the fattiness. I can close my eyes now and so easily find myself there, in the back garden at the age of 12 or 13: the smoky scent in the air, the uncomfortable plastic garden chair, the gentle warmth on my skin from the Sunday sun, my raucous family, and then me, silently working my way through a pile of salty lamb chops, using that salad for an acid kick.

This meal of my youth is deceptively simple, but it shares the three key building blocks of acid, texture, and contrast. In this way, it is not unlike the first dish I had at the legendary Marylebone restaurant The Providores, when I started working for Peter Gordon many moons ago and he served me a pork, chilli, coconut and gapi snack on a betel leaf with crispy shallots and tamarillo. My young, impressionable, fresh-out-of-college mind exploded, even if at least three of the things listed I had never heard of before.

The waiter recommended we roll it up and eat it. If there was ever a party in my mouth, that was the moment. The tastes were electric: there was crunch from shallots, and smooth pork, almost pâté-like in texture, flavoured with punchy gapi (fermented shrimp paste) and soothed with coconut milk, plus sweetness from the tamarillo, a fresh note from coriander (cilantro), and all finished with the perfect chilli heat lingering on my tongue. It was a taste sensation I will never forget. I ate that casual 'snack' almost 12 years ago, and the memory remains as vivid on my palate as if I ate it just yesterday.

Dishes don't have to be complicated but, in my mind, to make them sing they do need to have those key components: acid, texture, contrast. Keep these three in mind, understand them, play by their rules (and become confident enough to break those rules, once in a while), and you will be well on your way to creating magic.

ACID

Acid at the Base

Ask any chef or passionate cook you know, cooking from within any cultural heritage, and they'll probably be able to tell you the moment, dish or memory that made them realize how absolutely essential acid is to cooking. It is everywhere, in every style of cooking. A rich roast chicken, dripping with the fattiness only a happy chicken can provide, will need half a lemon stuffed inside its cavity. A Southeast Asian broth, rich with bubbling, creamy coconut milk, will be spiked with lime. Chilli-glazed barbecue wings, sticky and pungent, will have vinegar in the sauce. A hearty and filling ragout, with chunks of beef, will have been slow cooked with wine.

All of these dishes contain salt, heat, sweetness, texture, contrast, richness, umami. This plethora of tastes and experiences is what makes a dish come alive in your mouth. But what makes you want to go back to it, bite after bite, is the acid. The acid marries all of the different sensations, ties them down, lifts them, relieves them periodically and allows them to sing again. That is moreishness. It is what makes good food truly great. Next time you eat a dish, whether prepared by yourself or by someone else, look out for that acid. Let your palate explore the highs and lows and identify which component makes you want to go back for more.

Acid as Balance

Most often, acid makes an appearance in recipes as a balancing agent. Balance is at the heart of a good dish, and an easy way to start thinking about how dishes are put together is to think of counterbalances to everything you add.

'Fat is flavour' is possibly the sentence I sling around my kitchen most often – perhaps only just pipped to the post by 'tidy bench, tidy mind' (although that one I just mutter under my breath). But fat on its own doesn't work. Imagine taking a chunk of beef fat, curing it in a salt and sugar mix (leaving it for a bit), and then eating it straight-up like that. You may say: 'interesting', or 'nice exercise in using all of the animal', or 'what were you thinking'? But you won't last very long, perhaps one bite, if you can bear it, maybe two.

Now take a cabbage, which you have lovingly roasted and glazed with verjus (unripe grape juice that makes your cheeks pucker) while it roasts into something beautiful. Cut the aforementioned beef fat into small pieces and cook them down so they are nice and crunchy, and sprinkle it over the cabbage. The acidity inherent to the verjus and even in the cabbage itself is a beautiful counterbalance to the rich, almost overwhelming, fattiness of the beef. With this acidity, something that is almost unpalatable transforms into the most delicious thing you've had in a while, and the 'a-ha' moment of 'why didn't I think of this before?'

Acidity brightens up flavours that, on their own, may be a bit undefined. Take beans, a staple of the kitchen. On their own they don't naturally inspire cheers of delight – they're a bit grainy, a bit beige, a bit boring. Add them into a salad with some onions and a good hit of lemon and beans become your best friend: texturally interesting, a lovely earthiness, an absolute crowd-pleaser.

Acidity also balances out the cloying nature of sweetness and lifts it up – think of any good sweet and sour sauce you've ever had. It is in the counterweight of one element to another that you find the balance needed to take your dish to the next level.

No Two Acids Are the Same

Acid can come from a multitude of sources. You can introduce tang to dishes with sea vegetables (such as samphire), tomatoes, spices including amchur (dried mango powder), and pickled or salted vegetables such as sauerkraut. There are also levels of natural acidity in various salad leaves, king among them being sorrel. There is even acid to be had in cheeses like feta or parmesan.

But, I have a few go-tos that I come back to time and again. Chief of these is the lemon. This is my inheritance: lemon is an unmissable part of the Cypriot meal. Any self-respecting backyard in Cyprus has its own lemon tree, and Cypriots eat lemon with almost every meal, whether as part of the dish itself or served as wedges at the table. This is the palate my mother grew up with, and my grandmother before her, and, despite growing up in the UK (a far less Mediterranean sort of island), it is the palate I too developed at an early age. For me, lemon works best fresh and added at the table, as a sort of acidic seasoning, a spur-of-the-moment addition, an add-as-you-go sort of thing. It pays to look for good, unwaxed lemons and always have a few knocking about. Cut them lengthwise and check them for pips, and just serve them as wedges for your guests to add to dishes that are meat-forward, or grilled on the barbecue, or any piece of fish for that matter. Adding juice to a recipe, and having a hard time getting that juice out? Attack the flesh with a fork, screw it back and forth in the lemon, and all that elbow grease will allow you to extract the most juice.

I love vinegars. They are great bookends for a dish: they work as part of a marinade and pickle, at the beginning of the cooking process, and they are great as a dash at the end, to lift up the layers of flavours, in a slowly cooked ragout, for example. Dressings really don't work without them (unless you've gone for another acidic agent such as lemon or lime). But even when it comes to pickles, such as the liquor on p.87, I tend to add another bit of vinegar right at the very end, as it provides the extra ping of sharpness needed for a pickle.

Tamarind is a very sour, different kind of acidity. It's especially found in Southeast Asian-inspired cooking, and most often comes as a brown, hard block. It's easy to use: cook down the block with some water, pass it through a sieve (filtering out the pips), and the remaining pulp can be used in dressings, mayonnaise, curries and more. It stores really well in the freezer, and I will often make a bigger batch and freeze it in smaller portions (in an ice-cube tray, for example), and that way I'll have a stash of it, ready to go. It really is versatile and rewards those that approach it with oodles of flavour.

Sumac is another generous acidic ingredient. Known to most as a spice, it is actually ground dried berries. I like to play around with sumac, especially when plating up as part of the final seasoning. It works brilliantly as a sort of acidic fairy dust on fried stuff. Sprinkle it on fish or a fritter, or anything dipped in breadcrumbs and deep fried – the acidic tanginess cuts through the rich fried-ness beautifully.

TEXTURE

The Workhorse That Is Texture

What we put in our mouths matters. Cookbooks are, of course, a true testament to this: millions of words written in homage to the food we put in our mouths, what we do to it before it gets there, and how it should affect us when it arrives at its destination.

In eating, you use your senses: sight, smell, taste and sound. Personally, I have a thing for shades of (caramelized) brown with their promises of nutty, buttery, rich flavours. I love the smell of frying garlic and it makes my mouth water instantly. I can never resist the taste of something sour and I will happily finish off a bowl of green sour plums on my own, with devastating effects to follow. And there is nothing more seductive than the insistent crackle and pop of pork belly skin fresh out of the oven. In preparing food, you certainly use the fifth sense, touch, too. I love getting hands-on with my food, and I really think a salad should only be dressed with your hands.

We don't touch our food that much once it's prepared. In many food cultures (but thankfully not exclusively so) we have taught ourselves it is better to shovel the food into our mouths using a foreign object – fork, chopstick, cocktail stick, spork. It's only once the food is in our mouths that we really touch a dish – and that touch is called mouthfeel.

Mouthfeel is a terribly unsexy word, though – I prefer texture. Texture comes in many forms: food can be hard or soft, brittle or crisp or spongy. Texture can be smooth or coarse, consistencies can be creamy or watery, or an ingredient can feel sticky when it sits on the side of your mouth.

Food without texture is simply less palatable and eating becomes boring. Next time you eat something and are a little dissatisfied, think back and try to list the textures. Foods that are too soft, or too hard, or too chalky or, indeed, any of these textures without something else to contrast with, will leave us underwhelmed.

Texture
at the Core

Croutons are hands-down my favourite crunchy texture, ever. I feel a temptation, which I try to resist, to make them a part of dishes in which they traditionally do not belong.

Again, I reckon croutons might be a gene thing. In her heyday, my Nene in Cyprus would make fresh baharat-spiced bread every week. (She is a baker to this day; although, at 91, at a somewhat slower speed, albeit with the same precision and brilliance.) Baharat is a spice blend which mixes warm elements like cinnamon with the spiciness of cloves and mahlep (ground cherry stone). Nene has two clay wood-fired ovens (one big, one small) and, when we were younger and visiting Cyprus, my sisters and I would sit underneath the vines near the ovens, patiently waiting for the bread to be ready. As soon as it was cooked, we would break it open and smear lashings of butter all over it. The smell of that bread was completely addictive, and takes me right back to summers in Cyprus whenever we bake the same recipe in my restaurant in Central London.

From that weekly batch of bread, Nene would also make her peksimet (croutons). She would simply break up the bread once cool enough to handle, to make various oddly shaped and oddly sized little chunks. She would then put these bread chunks back in the now cooled oven to dry them out. By the time dusk rolled around, the peksimet would be ready. These would be eaten straight up for extra crunch along with lunch or dinner with fried red mullet, for example, along with a zingy salad of tomatoes and parsley. Or, if you weren't quite that hardcore (or didn't have your own teeth, like my grandfather), then you would wet them with some water to soften them up.

As a young, enthusiastic chef, looking to prove myself, I had a eureka moment. I realized that the best part of these peksimet at lunch or dinner in my younger days was the way in which the salad dressing on the plate would slowly soak into the bread chunks, and the croutons would still be crispy in the middle but with edges slightly softened. They would absorb the luscious dark olive oil and the salt and the flavours of the salad, and a peksimet would be hands-down my last forkful of the meal – the very best saved for the very end.

In this way, the crouton becomes an essential sidekick who does not feel the need to take the limelight. It is quite happy in its supporting role, soaking up other flavours but also providing the changes in mouthfeel, which means we move the tongue around more, enjoy the chewing, and experience the flavours one by one, apart, and then finally together.

Texture Everywhere

Of course, croutons are just one way of creating one texture. Chewiness can come in the form of dried fruits, cured meats and certain breads. Slipperiness sounds unalluring but an oyster hits that textural note just so. A sticky glaze or dressing will cling to roasted vegetables and almost transform them into candy. Raw fruit and veg will provide different textures again – an apple that is crisp yet firm, peas that pop, kohlrabi with its moreish succulence, or mangoes so juicy they make you dribble.

I stopped to think to myself why I like crunch so much – and I don't think I'm the only one. I found some studies that suggest there is a caveperson part of our brain which responds very positively to a bit of crunch. Crunchy, after all, usually meant fresh and healthy when it came to vegetables, back in the day. I sometimes wonder whether this is why we go a bit cuckoo for the crispiness of freshly fried chicken.

Purées, of course, are the opposite of crunchy. Perhaps we feel something completely different when we are eating a purée. Perhaps we love a purée because we know this vegetable has had loads of time spent on it; it has been dunked in butter, cooked long and tenderly, caramelized just so, mashed with vigour, whizzed, warmed, and generally loved.

Purées are silky and creamy and are a lovely way of transforming the textural fate of a vegetable. Take cauliflower, which is despised by many a child and adult, I think, because it so easily lends itself to being boiled to an absolute mush by well-intentioned spouses and parents. A cauliflower works beautifully sliced raw, as a pickle, as florets roasted or steamed, barbecued (the best), or in a purée. Here, you could go natural with the cauliflower cooked gently in butter (p.52), or caramelize the cauliflower before puréeing for a completely different flavour profile (p.52). The purée is a beautiful and versatile addition to your arsenal, and works to great contrasting effect with crunchy textures.

CONTRAST

Seriously Indebted to Contrast

Contrast, finally, is what transforms an ingredient into a journey, a culinary voyage. You hop from one forkful to another, exploring the contrasting flavours, textures, acids and temperatures. Acid is great, but never on its own. It needs something non-acidic or fatty or silky or creamy to cut through, or contrast with. Crunchy fried chicken is great, but pair fried chicken with a sticky, slippery sauce and you are on your way to food stardom.

Perhaps the best way of showing the importance of culinary contrast is its very real repercussions for one particular dish. It could be any dish, but while we're here we may as well go with one that you can have a crack at, at some point: winter fattoush and tamarind-glazed short rib (p.222).

Let's talk about fattoush – or fattush, fatush, fattoosh, or fattouche, depending on where you're from. A traditional fattoush will contain tomatoes, cucumber, lettuce, radish, onion, herbs, perhaps some purslane, and last but not least, pitta croutons. This is what the salad is named for, *fa* meaning 'crush' or 'crumb' in Arabic. The salad is bound with an olive oil-based dressing, with either lemon juice or vinegar and, crucially, tangy sumac. I am indebted to this traditional version, and my recipe is most certainly a tip of the hat to this classic.

In my case, I've gone with cucumber, cavolo nero, radish, spring onion, radicchio, chicory (endive), parsley, mint, croutons, pistachios, and pears; with parsley oil and a bit of yoghurt; slow-cooked, tamarind-glazed short rib; and sumac dressing with tons of lemon and garlic.

We have an abundance of texture, top of the list being the crunch of those croutons supporting juicy pears and a lovely silkiness from the parsley oil. The flavours from the pungent onion, fragrant herbs, and the bitterness of the radicchio and chicory all sit at different angles to each other. There are colours jostling on the plate, from olive green to herbaceous green, from bright red to deep maroon, from inviting golden brown croutons to golden glazed rib. There is acid, not only from the lemon and sumac in the dressing, but also in the dollops of yoghurt. The acidic creaminess of the yoghurt is a nice change to the crunchiness of the fresh vegetables, and its fridge-cold temperature cools the tongue after the sweet-sour warmth of the short rib.

I've used a variety of words to describe exactly what is going on, but really it is quite easy: contrast, contrast, contrast. No one ingredient works without the way it contrasts with another. Flavour comes from the way one experience is propped up by the other, how they push each other around in your mouth but never elbow each other out. The acid, the texture, and ultimately, the contrast, work in harmony.

Contrast Made Simple

Sounds complicated? It isn't really. Finding and creating contrast is a skill that can be learned. Tasting is your chief aid in this pursuit, and I recommend you taste as much as you can. Play around and see what appears. Find what contrast you like in particular, and don't be afraid to use it shamelessly, time and again. If it works, it works.

Like all chefs, I have a few staples. Sweet with savoury is one. Many of us have a natural aversion to overly sweet foods (like syrups or caramels), and by extension some people do not warm to sweet elements in savoury dishes. I think they are a match made in heaven. Just consider salted caramel. It works on an intrinsic level, where the sweet is balanced out and kept in check by the savoury. I love, for example, using Medjool dates in salads. Texturally, their squidginess sits nicely with a crispy crouton, for example. On a flavour level, they pair beautifully with a savoury element, such as salty feta cheese, or maybe some pork. Throw in an acidic element, in the form of a dressing, and you have just successfully integrated an ingredient previously relegated to sweet dishes only.

Temperature is another way of bringing contrast to a dish. I think temperature isn't played around with enough. Of course, applying temperature at the wrong moment or to the wrong ingredient can be incredibly unappetizing: a plate of wilted leaves served under the menu title of 'warm salad of something', or lamb fat, so beautiful when properly rendered down, that has gone cold. Temperature is a delicate thing and care is required. Take, for example, the layers of temperatures in the glazed Jerusalem artichokes with za'atar dressing (p.242). Warm, glazed and grilled artichokes are tossed with ingredients that are room-temperature. Radicchio, which has a juicy bitterness, earns its place because it is sturdy enough to support the warmth of the sticky artichokes. Crisp lavash bread is layered into the dish like little platforms to keep warm and cold elements separate. There's a hot purée served on the side of the plate, to prevent any more delicate ingredients wilting. Hot and cold contrast perfection.

My other go-tos are inevitably scattered through the parts of this foundational chapter that touch on acid and texture. Fat and acidity: a contrast made in heaven. Acidity and sweetness: really, really good. Crunchy croutons with edges going soft with salad dressing: yes, please. Onion pungency with sweet dates: always. Cold bread, hot butter. Coconut milk, chilli heat. Warm short rib, cold yoghurt. Savoury fatty lamb chops, sweet acidic lemons. I could go on.

BRINGING IT ALL TOGETHER

Bringing It All Together

The three foundations (acid, texture and contrast) that I have covered in the previous pages may seem like a lot of balls to juggle and hold in the air at the same time. But, I invite you to take this journey with me. It requires a bit of patience on your part, but it really is worth it. Start slow. Attempt some of the simpler dishes, and with every ingredient try to think about what they (acid, texture, contrast) bring to the plate. Learn the techniques in the recipes, get comfortable with them and build up muscle memory. If you are eating someone else's food, take a moment to identify the different components. Does the dish work? Why? What is it that makes it sing? Does it not work? What element is lacking, and what would you add? Of course, if this is a dinner party and you are the guest, perhaps perform this calculation in your head. Hosts probably won't take kindly to you going on about acid, texture and contrast at the dinner table and brandishing a notebook at the end of each course.

Before you know it, you will be well on your way to redefining your cooking. You will have the fundamental building blocks that will turn any dish into the star of the show. Give it time, and you will have the knowledge and know-how, and crucially, the inspiration to be able to replace my suggested ingredients with whatever you have in your store cupboard or fridge.

This is more than a cookbook. This is confidence. Knowing you can throw together a stellar dish — whatever the weather, the situation, or the direction of the world at large — is a skill that is more important than ever before.

TWO IDEAS & INSPIR- ATIONS

GLAZES

Vegetable Glaze

One of the first vegetable dishes I was taught at cooking college was Vichy carrots: essentially, glazed carrots. In this classic cooking method, you cook the carrots in water, butter and sugar, and sometimes a bit of spice, reducing the liquid down to a syrup to coat them in. It is a delicious and simple way of cooking vegetables, but I like adding in an extra step by grilling the vegetables after cooking them and then putting them back into the glaze.

This adds an extra level of smokiness. Try this glaze with Jerusalem artichokes, celeriac (celery root), onions, turnips, pumpkin or cabbage. The volumes here might sound like a lot, but by the time you've cooked your vegetables, the glaze will reduce down again by another half, and you can reuse it. It will store happily in the fridge for 6 weeks, just top it up with a little more water and reduce back down when you next cook.

Makes 1L (35fl oz) V

1L (35fl oz) water

250g (9oz) unsalted butter, diced

190g (6¾oz) demerara (turbinado) or caster (superfine) sugar

4 cardamom pods, crushed

4 star anise

Place all the ingredients into a pan and gently bring up to the boil. Turn the heat down to a simmer and cook for 5 minutes.

The liquor is now ready to use to cook your vegetables. Once your vegetables are cooked, reduce the liquor down to a syrup consistency and pour over the vegetables.

Verjus Glaze

Verjus is essentially raw grape juice. It has high levels of acidity and works very well in syrups and various sauces. In this recipe, it basically creates a posh version of the vegetable glaze.

The sugar and butter work in perfect harmony with the verjus to create an acidic, sweet glaze with plenty of beautiful viscosity. You can purchase verjus online or at a large wine store.

Makes 1L (35fl oz) V

750ml (26fl oz) verjus (verjuice)
250g (9oz) unsalted butter, diced
200g (7oz) demerara (turbinado)
  or caster (superfine) sugar
4 cardamom pods, crushed
4 star anise

Place all the ingredients into a pan and gently bring up to the boil. Turn the heat down to a simmer and cook for 5 minutes.

The liquor is now ready to use to cook your vegetables. Once your vegetables are cooked, reduce the liquor down to a syrup consistency and pour over the vegetables.

Tamarind Glaze

Tamarind is one of my favourite ways to bring acidity to a dish. In fact, it is probably more sour than acidic but acts in that same lip-puckering way a good acid does.

Making your own tamarind pulp is very easy. Simply take 2 blocks (400g/14oz) of tamarind, break them up into a pan and cover with water. Place over a low–medium heat and cook for 30 minutes or until you see the seeds have all separated and the pulp is a purée consistency.

While still hot, push the mix through a fine sieve (strainer) – this will take a bit of effort.

Discard the seeds and scrape every last bit of the remaining pulp into a container. Store in the fridge (for up to six weeks), or pour into ice-cube trays and freeze. Keep searching through this chapter for more ideas to use up your tamarind pulp, or turn to page 222 for tamarind-glazed short rib.

Makes 200g (7oz) VG

150g (5½oz) tamarind pulp
50g (1¾oz) dark brown sugar
2 Tbsp sherry vinegar

Place the ingredients in a pan over a medium–high heat and simmer for 10 minutes, stirring occasionally.

CRISPY THINGS & TOPPINGS

Salt & Pepper Walnuts

This is a great way to add seasoning and sweetness to nuts, and the end product is a bit like those amazing bar snacks you have in posh hotels. Use any nuts you would like. You can add spices like paprika, cumin, fennel, turmeric or coriander, and seeds like nigella or sesame. This is great for a crunchy texture in salads, or as garnish for buffalo mozzarella or a slab of feta along with a zingy dressing.

Serves 6–8 V

1 large egg white
40g (1½oz) icing (powdered) sugar
1 tsp sea salt flakes (kosher salt)
10 turns black pepper from a mill
165g (5¾oz) walnuts

Heat the oven to 170°C/150°C fan/325°F/gas mark 3.

Whisk the egg white until a little frothy and then whisk in the icing (powdered) sugar, salt and pepper. Coat the walnuts in this mix and then scatter over a baking sheet lined with baking paper in one even layer. Place into the oven and bake for 20 minutes, stirring every 5 minutes, or until the nuts are golden and crisp.

Buttered Crumbs & Sour Shallots

These crumbs are a great little trick to have up your sleeve to give an extra textural dimension to a dish. They work well with any sort of soups, stews, salads, egg dishes or even scattered over a pile of roasted vegetables.

Serves 4 V

70g (2½oz) unsalted butter
75g (2½oz) panko breadcrumbs
1 Tbsp banana shallot, finely diced
1 Tbsp vinegar (red, white, apple cider or moscatel)

Heat the oven to 170°C/150°C fan/325°F/gas mark 3.

Melt the butter and pour over the breadcrumbs. Whisk or use your hands to incorporate the butter. Season the crumbs with fine salt and scatter them onto a baking sheet lined with baking paper in one even layer, then place into the oven for 10–15 minutes, stirring every 5 minutes, or until they are a light golden brown colour and crisp. Leave to cool.

Meanwhile, combine the shallots and vinegar and leave to marinate for at least 10 minutes. Drain and mix into the crumbs and serve immediately.

Dukkah

Dukkah (or duqqa) is a spice mix originating in the Middle East. Hunks of bread are dipped in olive oil first and then into dukkah (the thought of which makes me salivate).

You could eat it in the traditional way, or you can sprinkle it over anything that needs a little perking up. I really love it with eggs (in particular eggs that have been boiled for exactly 6 minutes and therefore have the softest, creamiest yolk). You could also slow-roast some aubergines (eggplants), scoop out the flesh and chop it up with lots of herbs and garlic, mix it with olive oil and lemon juice, plate it and then sprinkle over generous amounts of this dukkah.

Makes 100g (3½oz) VG

50g (1¾oz) hazelnuts
3 Tbsp white or mixed
   sesame seeds
½ tsp cumin seeds
1 tsp coriander seeds
1 tsp fennel seeds
sea salt flakes (kosher salt)

Toast the hazelnuts and sesame seeds as instructed on page 49; in a separate pan, toast the spices. Leave to cool. Once everything has cooled, blitz the hazelnut and sesame seed mix in a food processor to a coarse crumb. Grind the spices, with a pestle and mortar, to a powder but retain a little texture – this is the texture I like, but you could also leave them a little chunkier or very fine. Combine and season with sea salt flakes (kosher salt) to taste. Store in an airtight container and use within 2 weeks.

Crispy Chickpeas

Warning: these are addictive. You could toss them in spices once cooked for extra fragrance (1 tsp smoked paprika, ½ tsp onion powder and ½ tsp ground coriander), or just with some good old curry powder. These are perfect for cocktail parties and for scattering over dips and salads.

Makes 350g (12oz) VG

1 x 400g (14oz) can chickpeas
   (garbanzo beans), drained
   and rinsed
extra-virgin olive oil
fine salt

Heat the oven to 200°C/180°C fan/400°F/gas mark 6.

Dry the chickpeas (garbanzo beans) thoroughly in a clean dish towel and discard any skins that come loose. Place in a bowl and coat with a little olive oil and fine salt. Lay out in one even layer onto a baking sheet lined with baking paper. Place into the oven and bake for 20–25 minutes, stirring every 5 minutes, or until they are crispy. Leave to completely cool before packing in an airtight container (if there is anything to pack away). These chickpeas will keep for up to 5 days.

Croutons

The idea behind a crouton is to preserve stale bread – any bread for that matter, from sourdough, pitta and ciabatta, right through to focaccia and rye.

Croutons that soak up the juices from a plate of food are the dream. There are two methods I like to use to make croutons:

1

Heat the oven to 180°C/160°C fan/350°F/ gas mark 4. Take your stale bread and cut or tear into 2–3cm (1in) pieces, drizzle with a little olive oil and sea salt flakes (kosher salt) and scatter in one even layer over a baking sheet. Place into the oven for 15–20 minutes or until golden brown and crisp. Check the progress of the croutons every 5 minutes – the ones on the outside might be ready sooner than those in the centre.

2

Fill a large frying pan (skillet) around a quarter of the way up with fat (clarified butter, ghee, duck, beef or whatever you'd prefer) and place over a medium-low heat. Cut or tear the stale bread into 1–2cm (½–¾in) pieces and place into the hot fat, ensuring the bread is all in one layer. If you like, at this point you could add in a crushed clove of garlic and a sprig of rosemary or thyme. Cook the croutons for 10–15 minutes, stirring every so often, until they are golden and crisp. Drain through a sieve (strainer) and then onto paper towels to absorb excess fat. Season with sea salt flakes (kosher salt)

Spiced Granola

Use the granola to add crunchy texture to soups, small plates or salads.

Makes 400g (14oz) V

1 Tbsp Kyseri spice mix (p.56)
1 heaped Tbsp honey
125ml (4fl oz) extra-virgin olive oil
2 egg whites
1 Tbsp sea salt flakes (kosher salt)
200g (7oz) puffed grains such
 as oats, wheat, spelt, quinoa,
 brown rice, millet or buckwheat
20g (¾oz) sesame seeds
60g (2¼oz) sunflower seeds
60g (2¼oz) pumpkin seeds
60g (2¼oz) flaked almonds

Heat the oven to 180°C/160°C fan/350°F/gas mark 4 and prepare the Kyseri spice mix as on page 56.

In a bowl, whisk together the honey, oil, egg whites, spice mix and salt to incorporate. Add the rest of the ingredients and stir to combine thoroughly. Line two large baking sheets with baking paper and spread the mix out evenly. Place into the oven and bake for 10–15 minutes, stirring halfway through, or until golden brown. Leave to cool and pack away into an airtight container for up to 2 weeks.

Spice Paste & Spiced Crumbs

Marinate cuts of meat or oily fish in this spice paste, barbecue or roast them, and thank me later. The crumbs are used in the recipe for avocado, brown shrimp, candied lemon and spiced crumbs on page 133 but would also be lovely sprinkled over any sort of eggs or slow-cooked stews. You can find Turkish mild pepper paste (tatli biber salçasi) in Turkish supermarkets or online, or if you really can't find it, tomato paste will do.

Makes 180g (6¼oz) V

For the spice paste
1 head (approx. 65g/2½oz) garlic, peeled
2 Tbsp olive oil
10g (¼oz) fine salt
30g (1oz) ground fenugreek
10g (¼oz) cumin seeds, toasted and ground
30g (1oz) paprika
80g (2¾oz) Turkish mild pepper paste (tatli biber salçasi)

For the crumbs
125g (4½oz) unsalted butter
150g (5½oz) panko breadcrumbs

Place the garlic, olive oil and salt into a blender with 1–2 Tbsp water and blitz to a smooth purée. Pour into a bowl and whisk in the rest of the spice paste ingredients. Store in an airtight container in the fridge for up to 3 months.

To make the crumbs, heat the oven to 170°C/150°C fan/ 325°F/gas mark 3. Melt the butter along with 1 Tbsp of the spice paste and whisk together. Take off the heat and whisk in the breadcrumbs, or use your hands (although disposable gloves would be advisable), until the spiced butter disperses through the crumbs evenly. Scatter onto a baking sheet in one even layer and place into the oven for 10–15 minutes, stirring every 5 minutes. Once they are a slightly deeper orange colour and crisp they are ready.

Crispy Lavash

Lavash is a very thin flatbread, often used to wrap up glorious morsels of grilled meat – it is the Middle Eastern version of tortillas, steamed pancakes (think Peking duck), tacos, scallion pancakes, and Ethiopian injera. We humans love wrapping up our meat in something doughy.

I like crisping up lavash and using it as a crunchy texture in dishes and salads. You can buy lavash in most Middle Eastern supermarkets; otherwise tortillas will work.

Grill the lavash on a hot barbecue or griddle pan – if you have neither, brown them a little in a dry hot frying pan (skillet). Once the breads have begun to colour and char, place them directly onto the rack of a preheated oven at 180°C/160°C fan/350°F/gas mark 4 for 5–10 minutes, flipping midway through, or until crispy. Leave them to cool and then break into large shards and store in an airtight container. They will keep for about 2 weeks.

Crispy Shallots & Garlic

You can buy very good Southeast Asian crispy shallots (most Asian supermarkets will sell these, and most local and national supermarkets usually have a version, too). Here is a recipe, if you do want to make them yourself.

Either way, they're put to good use throughout this book.

I'd be inclined to make my own crispy garlic, as it's far less time consuming.

Shallots

Finely slice banana shallots (2 shallots is enough for 4 people) into 5mm (¼in) rounds, using a mandoline or a sharp knife, and separate out the layers. Place a small deep pan on the stove and fill one-third to halfway up with a neutral oil. Add the shallots to the oil from cold, and fry until golden brown and crispy, stirring occasionally. Immediately take the shallots out of the oil and drain on paper towels, then season with fine salt while hot.

Garlic

Finely slice garlic cloves (2 garlic cloves should be enough for 4 people) carefully, using a mandoline or a sharp knife. Place a small deep pan on the stove and fill a third to a halfway up with a neutral oil. Add the garlic to the oil from cold. Carefully stir the garlic to ensure they don't stick together and watch them until they turn golden brown. Immediately take the garlic out of the oil and drain on paper towels, then season with fine salt while hot.

Toasting Nuts, Seeds & Spices

As a general rule of thumb, I prefer to toast nuts in the oven, and seeds and spices in a pan. As nuts are larger they need a more rounded heat, which the oven provides, whereas seeds and spices require a more direct heat from a pan to release their fragrance and oils. I tend to toast nuts as and when I need them, unless I am feeling particularly organized or if I am preparing 'Selin's salad bar' (see pages 103–4), in which case I will toast a few handfuls to have on hand.

Toasting and then grinding your spices is definitely worth it. The store-bought ground spices tend to be a little dull in flavour. Having said that, if you want to save on time they will do just fine. I often toast 3–4 Tbsp of the spices I use regularly and then grind them up to use in the recipe I am making at the time. I'll then have a little bit left for the next few uses.

Nuts

Toast at 190°C/170°C fan/375°F/gas mark 5 for 5–12 minutes. The timing really depends on the sort of nut you are toasting, but check to see if they have a little colour and fragrance after 5 minutes. If not, keep checking every 2 minutes. Depending on your taste preference you may enjoy the nuts slightly lighter or darker. Personally, I prefer walnuts, pecans and pistachios to have a deep toasty flavour, whereas something like hazelnuts (which have a strong dominant flavour) I will only toast lightly. Pine nuts do well with a light toasting to preserve their delicate flavour. Once completely cool, pack away in an airtight container for up to 2 weeks.

Sunflower and pumpkin seeds

Heat a large frying pan (skillet) over a medium heat for 30 seconds and then add in a drizzle of olive oil followed by the seeds (no more than one layer of seeds) and a good pinch of sea salt flakes (kosher salt). Toast them in the pan for 30–90 seconds, moving them regularly until they pop and colour a little. Immediately take them out of the pan and drain them on some paper towel. Leave them to cool and store in an airtight container. They will keep for up to a week.

Spices

Heat a large frying pan (skillet) over a medium heat for 1 minute and then add the spices (no more than one layer) and keep moving around in the pan for 30–90 seconds or until you can smell the fragrance, at which point immediately take the spices out of the pan. Leave them to cool completely and then grind to a powder in a spice grinder or with a pestle and mortar. If you prefer more texture, just lightly crush the spices. Pack away in an airtight container. They will last a couple of weeks.

PURÉES

A rule of thumb to remember for purées is that the more things you add to a purée, the more you will take away from the natural flavour of the ingredient you are puréeing. Less really is more. Purées can seem a little cheffy, but they are in fact a simple way of providing a silky, soft and unctuous texture to a dish, potentially elevating it from nice to exceptional.

If you are lucky enough to have one, a good high-speed blender will do all the work for you and produce a silky-smooth purée. If you don't have one, I would recommend you blend the purée as fine as your machine will take it and then push it through a fine sieve (strainer) to take out any lumps (unless you like that texture, in which case, leave the lumps in).

Black Garlic Purée

Black (aka aged) garlic is readily available these days. I like this purée for its decadence and its striking appearance. You can also blitz up a whole head of black garlic with lemon or vinegar, a big splash of olive oil and some herbs to use as a dressing for vegetables, salads or over a slow-roast piece of lamb.

Makes 200g (7oz) VG

1 head black garlic, peeled
25g (1oz) dark brown sugar
1 Tbsp soy sauce

Place the garlic, sugar and 200ml (7fl oz) water in a pan and bring up to a simmer. Cook gently for 15 minutes. Take the pan off the heat, add the soy sauce and blitz in a blender into a fine purée.

Natural or Caramelized Purée

You can make a purée out of almost any vegetable. You just have to decide whether you would like a lighter purée or one that has a caramelized flavour profile. If you're going for the latter, cauliflower, celeriac (celery root), Jerusalem artichoke and onions work particularly well. This is a general recipe, but quantities vary depending on the water content of the vegetable.

Makes 450–550g (16–20oz) V

500–600g (1lb 2oz–1lb 5oz)
   vegetable of your choice
125–150g (4½–5½oz)
   unsalted butter
neutral oil
fine salt
double (heavy) cream

Slice your vegetable into even-sized thin pieces. If you have a food processor with a slicing attachment or a mandoline, I suggest you use that for the most consistent results.

Place a large wide-based pan over a medium heat and add the butter along with a little splash of a neutral oil.

For a natural purée: add the vegetable slices to the pan and season with fine salt. Coat everything in the butter and cook for 5 minutes. Add around 125ml (4fl oz) water and place a lid on top. Continue to cook the vegetable, stirring every 1–2 minutes or until it is soft and can be crushed with a spoon. It's important to not let the vegetable get any colour, so if it starts to brown turn the heat down and add a little more water. Add 125ml (4fl oz) cream to the pan, bring up to the boil. Take the pan off the heat and strain the liquid into a bowl.

For a caramelized purée: add the vegetable slices to the pan, coat them in butter and season with fine salt. Cook for 30–40 minutes, stirring every 5 minutes, scraping the bottom of the pan as caramelized bits start to form. You want the veg slices to have turned a deep caramel colour and be soft enough to be crushed with a spoon. Strain off the excess butter and add a big splash of water and cream, around 125ml (4fl oz) of each. Bring to the boil and simmer for 1–2 minutes. Take the pan off the heat and strain the liquid into a bowl.

Whichever purée you decide on, while still hot, add the cooked vegetables into a blender and blitz as fine as it will go. You may find that you will need some of the cooking liquid to make the purée more fluid and silkier. Add a little at a time, blitz for a minute and then check to see whether the texture of the purée is to your liking. In some instances, you may need more liquid than you have so just add a little hot water if you feel the mixture is too stiff. Taste to see whether it needs more salt.

Purées

SPICE MIXES & OILS

Herb Oil

Basil and parsley, thanks to their full-on flavour, make my favourite herb oil. They also provide a sexy finish to a plate. If you want to make a straight parsley oil, then just use one big bunch of parsley and omit the basil. If you would prefer chive oil, then replace the basil with one big bunch of chives.

Makes 85ml (2¾fl oz) VG

100g (3½oz) basil stems and
    leaves, roughly chopped
25g (1oz) parsley, big stalks
    removed, roughly chopped
200ml (7fl oz) grapeseed oil

Prepare a bowl of iced water. Bring a pan of water up to a rapid boil, add the herbs and cook for 15 seconds. Take the herbs out and immediately dunk them in the iced water. Squeeze all the excess water from the herbs and roughly chop (reserve the iced water). Make sure you have really squeezed them and they are as dry as they can be.

Place the herbs into a high-speed blender with the oil and blitz, starting on the lowest setting for 30 seconds and then on to the fastest setting for 2–3 minutes, or until the herbs are as fine as they will go. Don't worry if the oil heats up through blending – this is a normal part of the process and helps the colour of the herbs release into the oil.

At this point you need to decide on whether to leave herby bits in the oil or strain them off. If straining, line a fine sieve (strainer) with muslin (cheesecloth) and place over a bowl that fits within the iced water bowl. Pour the oil mix into the lined sieve and leave to drip for 1–2 hours. If you are leaving the bits in, then simply place the oil into a bowl over the iced water to cool.

Store in a squeezy bottle or container in the fridge for up to 1 month.

Kyseri Spice Mix

This was our house spice mix at my London restaurant Kyseri. It has a warming flavour that pairs really well with poultry, meats, fish and vegetables. Try adding this to mayonnaise, thick yoghurt or cream cheese for a quick and delicious dip.

Makes 50g (1¾oz) VG

2 tsp coriander seeds

2 tsp cardamom pods, husks removed

2 tsp ground or freshly grated nutmeg

1 tsp cloves

1 tsp cinnamon

1 tsp ground ginger

1 tsp ground turmeric

1 tsp black peppercorns

Blitz all the spices together in a spice grinder or small blender, or grind using a pestle and mortar. Store in an airtight container and use within 4 weeks.

Garlic, Chilli & Sherry Vinegar Oil

Other vinegars can be used, but sherry vinegar has the most distinct flavour. Spoon over eggs or over a piece of roasted or steamed fish. Use dried chilli (red pepper) flakes if you can't find whole dried guindilla or guajillo chillies.

Makes 200ml (7fl oz) VG

3 long dried red chillies such as guindilla or guajillo

150ml (5fl oz) extra-virgin olive oil

4 garlic cloves, finely sliced

75ml (2¼fl oz) sherry vinegar

Place the chillies in boiling water for 5 minutes to rehydrate. Drain, leave to cool slightly and then slice into rounds.

Combine the olive oil and garlic in a large frying pan and fry over a medium–high heat until the edges of the garlic start to turn golden brown. Add the chilli, followed by the vinegar and turn off the heat. Cool completely, then store in an airtight container in the fridge for up to 3 weeks.

MARI-NADES & CURES

Marinated Oily Fish

This is a great way of marinating salmon, trout, mackerel, sardines, herring or tuna. You could simply serve the resulting fish with chopped chives or diced red onion and crusty bread. For sardines, mackerel and herring I would leave the skin on; for all others ask your fishmonger to remove the skin and cut any large fillets from fish like salmon or tuna into portions. Leftover marinade can be used as a dressing for salads or can be tossed through some warm vegetables as a side for seafood dishes.

Serves 2–4

500–700g (1lb 2oz–1lb 9oz) filleted fish
2 Tbsp fine salt
250ml (9fl oz) extra-virgin olive oil
3 Tbsp vinegar (red, white, apple cider or moscatel)
2 garlic cloves, crushed
2 sprigs of thyme
1 bay leaf, torn

Season both sides of the fish fillets evenly with the salt and place on a baking sheet and into the fridge for 12–24 hours. Using a paper towel, wipe the fish dry ready for the marinade.

Mix together the remaining ingredients and place into a shallow container that will allow the fish to sit in one layer. Cover the fish with the marinade, ensuring it is completely submerged in the oil – add more oil if necessary. Cover the container and place into the fridge. Ideally leave to marinate for 3–4 days before eating, but it will be ready after 24 hours.

Curing Meat & Fat

Cured fat will keep for ages in the fridge, so it's a really great ingredient to have in your arsenal. When finely diced and cooked it transforms into the most amazing little meaty croutons and reveals lots of lovely liquid fat. You can use the latter to sear meat, or sweat veggies for your next beef or lamb ragout. Sometimes I will go all-out and coat breadcrumbs in that rendered fat and then toast them in the oven until golden and crisp.

Curing salt can also be used to season meats for pan-frying and roasting, or you could cure lamb or pork chops for a maximum of 4 hours and then pan-fry or grill them for bacon-like chops.

For the curing salt
300g (10½oz) sea salt flakes
    (kosher salt)
300g (10½oz) fine salt
400g (14oz) demerara
    (turbinado) sugar
25g (1oz) dried oregano
    (wild oregano is best,
    if you can find it)

Items you can cure
Chunks of beef or lamb fat
Boned lamb breast to make
    lamb bacon
Pork or lamb chops

Place all of the curing salt ingredients into a food processor and blitz for 10–20 seconds to combine everything and break up the salt and sugar crystals a little.

For every 500g (1lb 2oz) of meat or fat, use approximately 15g (½oz) of curing salt. Coat the meat or fat liberally in the curing salt, place into a container, cover and place into the fridge for 7 days to cure (unless curing pork or lamb chops, which should be cured for a maximum of four hours). After 3 days turn the pieces of fat or meat over and change the container you are storing it in, to get rid of any excess moisture.

After 7 days wipe away any excess cure that hasn't dissolved. Lamb or beef fat will then be ready to use. If you are making lamb bacon, you will need to dry the meat in the fridge for 4–5 days before use. You can either hang the meat on a hook in the fridge (if you have space) or place the meat on a rack over a tray.

JAMS, CONDIMENTS & DIPS

Braised Garlic

Roasted garlic has a completely different taste to raw garlic. It sweetens and mellows in flavour immensely. Use this as a sauce (with a little butter stirred in at the end) and spoon over a chicken or pork chop, or pool inside a well of yoghurt and serve as part of a sharing spread for the most off-the-charts delicious dip you could imagine.

Makes 150g (5½oz) VG

1 head garlic, peeled
2 banana shallots, peeled
   and sliced into 1cm rounds
1 Tbsp pomegranate molasses
¼ tsp dried chilli (red pepper)
   flakes (pul biber, preferably)
½ tsp sumac
½ tsp dried oregano
2 Tbsp extra-virgin olive oil

Heat the oven to 180°C/160°C fan/350°F/gas mark 4.

Combine all the ingredients together in an ovenproof dish, with 2 Tbsp water and a pinch of fine salt. Cover with foil and place into the oven for 35 minutes or until the garlic is soft. Turn the oven up to 210°C/190°C fan/415°F/gas mark 6–7, remove the foil and continue to cook for a further 8–10 minutes or until the top of the garlic has browned a little.

Cashew Nut Condiment

Sometimes it's a bit hard to put a label on the things I cook – ingredients from around the world all end up crossing paths. Call it the Peter Gordon effect, I guess, aka the 'father of fusion'. I will not claim this one is a sambal, or a chutney, or a dukkah, but it is a condiment inspired by all of those things.

Makes 250g (9oz) VG

150g (5½oz) cashews, toasted
¼ tsp sesame oil
1½ Tbsp soy sauce
1 spring onion (scallion),
   finely sliced
½ lime, zested and juiced
100g (3½oz) desiccated
   (shredded) coconut, toasted
1 Tbsp black and white sesame
   seeds

Blitz the cashews in a food processor into a coarse crumb. Place into a bowl, add the rest of the ingredients and season with salt to taste. This will keep well in the fridge for 1–2 weeks.

Sherry Caramel

This caramel is delicious over ice cream. It's sweet and sour and has a complex flavour from the sherry. If you're not a dessert person, it is also immensely good with potatoes or cheese, or drizzled over vegetables and salads.

Makes 200ml (7fl oz) VG

135g (4¾oz) caster (superfine) sugar
250ml (9fl oz) sherry (fino, manzanilla or oloroso)
250ml (9fl oz) sherry vinegar

Combine the sugar and 200ml (7fl oz) water in a heavy-based pan and place over a medium heat. Cook for 5–10 minutes or until the sugar melts into a deep golden-brown caramel. Do not stir the sugar while cooking – just shake the pan to move around the sugar – or you risk crystallizing the caramel. Take the pan off the heat and carefully add the sherry and vinegar – be careful, it will spit as you do this! Put the pan back over a low heat and once any hard caramel pieces have dissolved, turn the heat up and cook until it resembles a syrup consistency.

If you are unsure as to whether the caramel is thick enough, put a little onto a plate, chill in the fridge or freezer for 5–10 minutes and then run your finger through it. If the mix stays apart it's ready; if it comes back together, then boil for another 2 minutes, turn off the heat and test again. Repeat until ready. If the caramel has gone too far and completely sticks to the plate then add a little splash of water and gently heat through to thin the mixture. Store in a container at room temperature for up to 3 months.

Lemongrass Caramel

Full-on fragrance and an impressive little trick
to have up your sleeve for drizzling over just
about anything when you are cooking with
flavours from the Far East. Again, it's fabulous
spooned over ice cream.

Makes 80ml (2½fl oz) VG

2 lemongrass
80g (2¾oz) palm sugar or
   light brown sugar
1–2 limes, juiced

*Bruise the lemongrass by whacking it with the back of your
knife, peel the outer layers off, and trim ¼ from the thinnest end.
(Reserve these trimmings for infusing in future broths and curries
– they store brilliantly in sandwich bags in the freezer.) Very finely
chop the lemongrass.*

*Place the sugar in a heavy-based pan over a medium heat. Cook
the sugar until it melts into a dark golden-brown caramel. Add
the lemongrass followed immediately by 3 Tbsp water and the
juice of 1 lime. Simmer for 5–10 minutes or until it resembles a
syrup consistency and any lumps have dissolved. Leave it to cool
for 15 minutes before tasting and add more lime juice if required.
It will keep well in the fridge for 3–4 weeks.*

Dried Shrimp & Citrus Peel Sambal

Sambals are absolutely delicious: condensed chilli-paste flavour bombs from Indonesia, Malaysia, Sri Lanka and Singapore. If you haven't tried one before, I suggest you do – there are hundreds of varieties to explore.

At the base of almost all of them, you'll find red chillies. Sambals often include all manner of acids (local citrus, tamarind), coconut, fish (dried shrimp, anchovies) and aromatics (ginger, garlic, onions, lemongrass).

Makes 450g (1lb)

80g (2¾oz) dried red chillies
20g (¾oz) dried shrimp
150g (5½oz) shallots (Thai red onions, preferably), roughly chopped
6 garlic cloves, roughly chopped
10cm (4in) ginger, roughly chopped
150ml (5fl oz) neutral oil
20g (¾oz) shrimp paste
80g (2¾oz) candied or mixed peel
45g (1¾oz) palm sugar or brown sugar
1 Tbsp tamarind pulp (p.40)
1–2 limes, zested and juiced

Pour boiling water over the dried red chillies and allow to steep for 10 minutes. Drain, cool and then remove the seeds. In another bowl, meanwhile, pour boiling water over the dried shrimp and leave for 10 minutes, before draining.

Blitz the chillies along with the shallots, garlic, rehydrated shrimp, ginger and 250ml (9fl oz) water in a blender or food processor until it comes together into a coarse purée.

Heat a large pan over a medium heat with half the oil, add the purée and season with fine salt. Cook for 30–40 minutes or until the mix thickens. Add the remaining oil, the shrimp paste, candied peel, sugar and tamarind pulp and turn the heat down to a low setting. Cook for up to 50 minutes or until the colour darkens and the oil splits from the purée. Once cool, add the lime juice and zest and taste to check if the mix needs salt or more lime. This will keep well, in a sealed container, in the fridge for up to 3–4 weeks.

Preserved & Candied Lemon

You can use these lemons as you would traditional preserved lemons, in salad dressings by dicing up the skin and mixing with olive oil and fresh lemon juice, or you can even add to softened butter with herbs and grated garlic, and smear under the skin of a whole chicken before roasting. Leave the lemons in the salt and they will be ready after 2 weeks. Don't forget to stir every 4 days or so, and always rinse thoroughly before use.

Makes 200g (7oz) VG

2 lemons, quartered
1 Tbsp fine salt
1 Tbsp sea salt flakes (kosher salt)
125g (4½oz) caster (superfine) sugar

In a bowl, combine the lemons and both salts. Using your hands, massage the salt into the lemon wedges and squeeze the wedges so they start to release their juice. Once everything is mixed well, place into a sterilized jar or container and cover the top of the lemons with a small piece of baking paper. Place into the fridge for 8 days, giving them a stir after 4 days.

Rinse the lemons under cold water and taste a little of the rind to see if it is very salty. If so, then submerge the lemons in cold water and leave them soaking, checking to taste the rind again every 30 minutes or so, and changing the water a few times. They should be highly salted but palatable.

Slice away the flesh of the lemons and discard, then finely dice the peel.

Combine 250ml (9fl oz) water and the sugar in a pan and gently bring up to the boil. Add the diced lemon and simmer for 15–20 minutes or until the liquid turns to a syrup. Leave to cool and store in a sterilized jar or container in the fridge for up to 8 weeks.

Muhammara

This is a traditional component of a Turkish spread or meze but originally hails from Syria. Most recipes will include roasted red (bell) peppers but I prefer without. I love it on toast with a sprinkling of chives and Maldon salt, or in a sandwich with grilled halloumi. Turkish pepper paste is available to buy online and in Middle Eastern supermarkets.

Makes 300g (10½oz) VG

150g (5½oz) walnuts, toasted
40g (1½oz) Turkish mild pepper
   paste (tatli biber salçasi)
120ml (4fl oz) extra-virgin olive oil
1 garlic clove, finely grated
½ tsp dried chilli (red pepper) flakes
   or powder (pul biber, preferably)
¼ tsp cumin seeds, toasted and
   ground
½ lemon, juiced
25g (1oz) pomegranate molasses
1 tsp caster (superfine) sugar

Once the walnuts have cooled from toasting, place them into a food processor and blitz to a coarse crumb. Place into a bowl with the rest of the ingredients and mix thoroughly. Season to taste using fine salt. Store in a container in the fridge for up to 3 weeks.

Miso Butter

Miso is a workhorse. Whichever kind you buy – white, yellow, red, brown, barley or soybean – does brilliantly in soups, glazed over aubergine (eggplant) and even in desserts with things like caramel. The saltiness of miso also lends itself very well to butter. Have this butter on hand and use on grilled steak, roast chicken, on piles of vegetables or tossed through some noodles with copious amounts of chopped coriander (cilantro).

Serves 6–8 V

250g (9oz) unsalted butter,
    room temperature
65g (2¼oz) miso (any kind)
25ml (2 Tbsp) mirin
1 Tbsp thyme leaves
½ lime, zested and juiced

Blend all of the ingredients together until well incorporated. This will keep well in the fridge for 4–5 weeks or in the freezer for 3 months.

Green Chilli Jam

If you love chilli, then having a jar of this knocking around can only be a good thing. It will pair very nicely with cheeses, eggs, seafood and meat. Ripple through sour cream, for a slightly cooling effect, and it will be a perfect dip for a bowl of tortilla chips.

Makes 400–500g (14–18oz) VG

100g (3½oz) green chillies, roughly chopped
300–350g (10½–12oz) green (bell) peppers, seeds removed and roughly chopped
3 banana shallots, roughly chopped
5 garlic cloves, roughly chopped
10cm (4in) ginger, peeled and roughly chopped
125ml (4fl oz) neutral oil
125g (4½oz) palm sugar, roughly chopped, or light brown sugar
1–2 limes, juiced

Place the chillies, peppers, shallots, garlic and ginger into a food processor and blitz to a coarse purée.

Heat the oil in a large pan over a medium heat and add the paste. Turn the heat down to low, and cook the paste for 1½–2 hours or until it has completely softened. It should look a very dull green colour.

Add the sugar and cook for a further 10 minutes. Take off the heat and add in the juice of 1 lime and taste. If the mix is very hot or you would like more acidity, then add the juice of the second lime, too.

Leave the jam to cool for 15 minutes and then tip into a warm sterilized jar or container and seal. Store in the fridge and use within 2–3 months.

Green Tomato Ketchup

I only discovered the joy of green tomatoes a few years ago. They're in season in the UK in late summer and now, frankly, I can't do without them. They are delicious sliced very thin and tossed through a salad or cooked down (as in this recipe) as a ketchup or chutney. Another great idea for green tomatoes is to char them over a barbecue or roast in the oven for 1–2 hours at 180°C/160°C fan/350°F/ gas mark 4, then finely chop or blitz them in a food processor, along with some coriander (cilantro), garlic, chilli, olive oil and lime juice, to make a salsa.

Use this ketchup with anything you would use a regular ketchup with.

Makes 250g (9oz) VG

500g (1lb 2oz) green tomatoes, roughly chopped
125ml (4fl oz) distilled vinegar
125g (4½oz) caster (superfine) sugar
1 star anise

Place all of the ingredients in a pan, stir and gently bring up to the boil. Turn down to a simmer and cook until the tomatoes are very soft and can be squashed with the back of a spoon. Strain the liquid off from the tomatoes and pick out the star anise. Place the tomato pulp into a high-speed blender and blitz as fine as it will go. Pass through a sieve (strainer), if you wish, for an extra smooth finish. Store in a sterilized jar in the fridge and use within 4–6 weeks.

Tomato Yuzu Jam

It was chef Peter Gordon who first introduced me to yuzu. Being an acid-addict, it was love at first sight (the yuzu, not Peter; we bat for opposite teams and I love Peter like a father).

Make a batch of this jam and pair it with cheese or just spread it on some hot buttered toast. It's also great with a wedge of cooked halloumi (p.98). You can buy yuzu juice online.

Makes 650g (1lb 7oz) VG

50g (1¾oz) tamarind pulp (p.40)
500g (1lb 2oz) ripe red tomatoes, roughly chopped
400g (14oz) granulated or caster (superfine) sugar
4 garlic cloves, finely grated
40g (1½oz) ginger, finely grated
2½ Tbsp yuzu juice

Prepare the tamarind pulp as on page 40.

Place all the ingredients, except the yuzu juice, into a pan and very gently bring to the boil, ensuring all the sugar is dissolved before the mix boils. Turn down to a rapid simmer and cook to 106°C/222°F. If you don't have a thermometer, take a little of the jam onto a plate when you think it's ready, chill in the fridge or freezer for 5–10 minutes and then run your finger through it. If the mix stays apart it's ready; if it comes back together, then boil for another 2 minutes, turn off the heat and test again. Repeat until ready. Add the yuzu and mix thoroughly. Leave the jam to cool for 15 minutes and then place into a warm sterilized jar and seal the top. This will keep for up to 6 months in a cool, dry, dark place unopened. Once open, store in the fridge and use within 3–4 weeks.

Gremolata-ish

A classic gremolata is just parsley, garlic and
lemon zest, but this is the Selin gremolata-ish
version. It's great on top of slow-cooked,
rich dishes, in particular, as it provides a little
refreshing relief.

Serves 4–6 VG

50g (1¾oz) flat-leaf parsley
1 garlic clove
1 lemon or lime, zested
½ Tbsp dried oregano
1 Tbsp thyme leaves
½ Tbsp dried chilli (red pepper)
   flakes (pul biber, preferably)

*Finely chop the parsley and garlic together, running your knife
through the mix many times, so it becomes very fine. Place into
a bowl and stir in the remaining ingredients. Serve immediately.*

Mayonnaise

Ensure everything is at room temperature for easier emulsification and use the best eggs.

This is a basic mayo which you can add all sorts to, including garlic, chilli, spices and herbs. You could even substitute some of the oil for some flavoured fat, from sausages like chorizo or merguez, or even a little bacon fat. Acidity can come from vinegars, citrus fruits or tamarind. Play around with the flavours and see what you come up with.

Makes 250g (9oz) V

1 egg
1 tsp Dijon mustard
1 Tbsp vinegar (red, white,
    apple cider, sherry or moscatel)
fine salt, to taste
250ml (9fl oz) neutral oil
    (grapeseed, groundnut
    or sunflower)
1 Tbsp Kyseri spice mix
    (p.56, optional)

Add the egg, mustard, vinegar, a little salt and the oil into a beaker or jug. Place a hand blender (stick blender) into the bottom, start blitzing and slowly pulling up the blender until everything is incorporated.

If you want to make this a spiced mayonnaise, simply add the Kyseri spice mix, and mix again.

Store in a container, in the fridge, for up to 1 week.

Hummus

Every self-respecting mum in Cyprus, Turkey and the Middle East has their own hummus recipe, the hummus recipe to beat all hummus recipes (my mum included). A dear Lebanese friend still reminds me of the first time I visited her house. My mum packed me off to this party with a tub of her homemade hummus; my friend's mum had also made hummus, and to this day there still remains some friction over whose hummus was better.

Smooth hummus is something we all aspire to, and if you went looking, you could find a hundred and one different suggestions to get the right consistency, from peeling the chickpeas (garbanzo beans) to adding bicarbonate of soda (baking soda). For what it's worth, here are my recommendations for the smoothest hummus ever (be wary of bringing it to dinner parties):

1. The chickpeas need to be the small, dried brown variety (not the bigger, whiter ones, and not the ones that have been sitting at the back of the shelf for several years). Find a good quality brand from a Middle Eastern country. That is where hummus comes from, after all.

2. Use a pressure cooker to cook them. You can do it without (although the cooking process will be a lot longer), but a pressure cooker will almost obliterate the chickpeas and make them as soft as they can be.

3. Use a high-speed blender (the one you use to make a smoothie), as these blenders are designed to blitz things as fine as possible. Serve the recipe opposite as is, or top with some cooked chickpeas, olive oil, parsley, sumac and paprika. You can also go all-out with a fully loaded hummus (p.196) of my (or your own) design. Serve with lots of warm pitta or crusty bread.

Serves 4–6 VG

250g (9oz) best-quality small,
    dried brown chickpeas
    (garbanzo beans)
1 tsp bicarbonate of soda
    (baking soda)
1 onion, cut into 4
1 carrot, cut into 4
1 celery stick, cut into 4
1 large or 2 small garlic
    cloves, finely grated
1 tsp pul biber or dried chilli
    (red pepper) flakes, optional
125g (4½oz) best-quality tahini
2–4 lemons, juiced (70g/2½oz)
3 Tbsp extra-virgin olive oil

Cover the chickpeas (garbanzo beans) with 5–7cm (2–3in) of water, stir in the bicarbonate of soda (baking soda) and leave overnight (or at least 12 hours). Drain the chickpeas, rinse under cold water and place into the pressure cooker along with the onion, carrot and celery. Add cold water to come two-thirds of the way up the pan. Place the lid on, ensuring it is secure, and place over a medium–high heat. Once you can hear the pan boiling, turn the heat down to its lowest setting and cook for 30 minutes. Turn the heat off and leave the pressure to settle for 10 minutes before releasing the pressure according to the instructions of your pressure cooker. Check the chickpeas are very soft, and if not, cook them for longer under pressure.

You will notice some of the skins will have floated to the top. To encourage this further, give the chickpeas a good stir to rough them up and then, using a slotted spoon, remove all the skins that float to the top (don't spend hours trying to remove every skin, just the ones that naturally come off).

Spoon the chickpeas (reserve some for garnish, if you like) into a high-speed blender along with 350ml (12fl oz) of the cooking liquid and a generous pinch of salt and start to blend. Discard the vegetables. After 1 minute stop the machine, scrape down the sides of the blender and check if you are happy with the consistency. If the mix seems thick and isn't blending easily, add enough cooking water to allow it to blend freely. Blitz for another 5–6 minutes, scraping down the sides of the blender halfway through. At this point you should have a very smooth chickpea purée – if not, blend for longer. Add the garlic and pul biber, if using, and continue to blend for 1 minute. Using a spatula scrape out the mix into a bowl and cover with a piece of baking paper to stop it forming a skin. Leave to cool to room temperature.

Whisk in the tahini, lemon and oil and adjust to your liking. A hummus recipe will never be exactly the same so taste it to see if it needs more salt, lemon, garlic, tahini or olive oil. I like it with not too much tahini and plenty of garlic and lemon. Store in a container, in the fridge, for up to 5 days.

DRESS-INGS

Black Olive Dressing

Be sure to get the best black olives you can get, as they are the heart of this dressing. It works brilliantly with watermelon, to dress a crunchy salad or even with meat and fish. This also works as a dip at the start of a meal with a pile of crusty bread.

Makes 200g (7oz) VG

120g (4¼oz) pitted black olives, thoroughly rinsed
1 Tbsp dried oregano or mixed herbs
2 Tbsp balsamic vinegar (use another vinegar if you don't have balsamic)
65ml (2¼fl oz) extra-virgin olive oil

Roughly chop the olives or blitz them in a food processor and place into a bowl. Whisk in the remaining ingredients. The dressing will keep well in the fridge for up to 3–4 weeks.

Citrus Dressing

A good citrus dressing is an essential recipe to perk up a bowl of leaves or greens, especially those requiring more acidity, such as kale.

Makes 200g (7oz) VG

1 lime, segmented
1 orange, segmented
1 lemon, segmented
1 Tbsp vinegar (red, white, apple cider or moscatel)
½ banana shallot, finely diced
1 small garlic clove, finely grated
2.5cm (1in) ginger, finely grated
150ml (5fl oz) extra-virgin olive oil

Squeeze the juice from the leftover citrus fruits after segmenting. Mix the vinegar and shallot and leave to stand for 20 minutes. Add the garlic, ginger, olive oil and citrus juice and whisk thoroughly. Cut each citrus segment into 3 and add to the bowl. Season with salt to taste. This will keep well in the fridge for up to 10 days.

Chilli Dressing

This dressing straddles Middle Eastern and Asian cuisines. You could replace the dried chilli (red pepper) flakes with freshly ground black pepper.

Makes 250ml (9fl oz)

1½ Tbsp dried chilli (red pepper)
   flakes such as urfa, pul biber
   or regular
2 Tbsp fish sauce
1½ Tbsp honey
2 Tbsp soy sauce
1 Tbsp coriander seeds,
   toasted and ground
1 Tbsp cumin seeds,
   toasted and ground
125ml (4fl oz) extra-virgin olive oil
1 lemon, juiced

Whisk, blend or shake the whole lot in a jar. The dressing will store well in the fridge for 3–4 weeks.

Sumac Dressing

Zingy and light, this dressing is perfect tossed through salad leaves but also works well with chilli-spiked dishes thanks to its almost cooling effect.

Makes 150ml (5fl oz) VG

125ml (4fl oz) extra-virgin olive oil
1 garlic, finely grated
1 lemon, juiced
1 Tbsp sumac

Whisk, blend or shake the whole lot in a jar. Season to taste. It will store well in the fridge for 2–3 weeks.

Pomegranate Dressing

Şalgam is fermented turnip juice, widely used in Turkey for dressings and pickles and is available in Middle Eastern supermarkets. It works here to add a little funk to the dressing.

This, combined with the highly sour and subtly sweet flavour of pomegranate molasses, lends itself to a variety of dishes, from cheeses to meat and fish.

Makes 200ml (7fl oz) VG

1 Tbsp vinegar (red, white,
   apple cider or moscatel)
3 Tbsp pomegranate molasses
2 Tbsp şalgam (optional)
140ml (4¾fl oz) extra-virgin olive oil
½ banana shallot, finely diced
½ garlic clove, finely grated
1 tsp thyme leaves
½ pomegranate, seeds picked

Whisk together the vinegar, pomegranate molasses and şalgam. While still whisking, slowly drizzle in the olive oil to emulsify the mix. Add the rest of the ingredients and season to taste with salt. Re-whisk or shake (in a jar) before using. It will store well in the fridge for 1–2 weeks.

Honey & Shallot Dressing

Dressings with honey can sometimes be overpoweringly sweet, but I think this version is well-balanced. The moscatel vinegar brings its own acidic sweetness, while shallot and thyme counter with savoury flavour. Take the time to try and dice the shallot as small as you can so it isn't too intrusive. If you are after an easy yet impressive dressing for a side salad, then this is my pick.

Makes 240ml (8fl oz) V

1 banana shallot, finely diced
2½ Tbsp honey
80ml (2½fl oz) moscatel vinegar
   (use another vinegar if you
   don't have)
90ml (3fl oz) extra-virgin olive oil
1 Tbsp thyme leaves

Whisk all the ingredients together or place in a jar and shake. Season to taste with salt. The dressing will store well in the fridge for up to 1 week.

Fermented Black Bean Dressing

Chinese fermented black beans (douchi) are very distinct and complex, and they really caught my attention for their versatility and as a flavour boost for the simplest of dishes. They're available at Asian supermarkets and online. I especially love this recipe with fish. Feel free to think outside the box – this dressing pairs really well with a huge variety of ingredients.

Makes 340ml (11¾fl oz) VG

2 garlic cloves
1 chilli
2 spring onions (scallions)
5cm (2in) ginger, peeled
160g (5¾oz) Chinese fermented
  black beans (douchi), rinsed
  under warm water
1 lime, zested and juiced
135ml (4½fl oz) neutral oil

Cut the garlic, chilli, spring onions (scallions) and ginger into chunks. Place into a blender along with the black beans, lime zest and juice and blitz to form a paste. Add the oil and blitz again. Taste and add more lime if need be. The dressing will store well in the fridge for 3–4 weeks.

Palm Sugar, Chilli & Lime Dressing

I adore this dressing for its acidic yet slightly sweet and fragrant flavour, and I make it at least once every few weeks. I crave it with roast meats, such as pork shoulder (p.219), whole roast duck or chicken. Tear chunks of the meat off, dip in the dressing and devour. Please do source proper palm sugar: when it's good, its toffee-like flavour is one you will become addicted to and want to use all the time.

Makes 100ml (3½fl oz)

45g (1¾oz) palm sugar
½–1 chilli, depending on
  how hot you like it
1 large or 2 small garlic cloves
4 Tbsp fish sauce
2 limes, juiced

In a small blender, blitz together all the ingredients. Taste and adjust with more sugar or lime if needed. It will store well in the fridge for up to 1 week.

Miso & Lemon Dressing

Miso has a deep, savoury, sweet yet fruity flavour due to its fermentation process. There are no limits to what I would pair it with. Used sparingly I believe this dressing will go with pretty much anything. Try cutting a selection of seasonal, crunchy vegetables and using it as a dip.

Makes 220ml (7½fl oz) VG

80g (2¾oz) white or brown
  miso paste
1 banana shallot, finely diced
1 garlic clove, finely grated
1 lemon, juiced
120ml (4fl oz) extra-virgin olive oil

Place all the ingredients in a pan and cook over a gentle heat, whisking occasionally, for 10–15 minutes or until the shallot has softened. Allow the mix to cool completely and then adjust with more lemon if needed. This will store well in the fridge for up to 2 weeks.

Yellow Bean Dressing

This dressing and cucumber are best friends, but beyond that you could also use it to dress finely sliced cabbage or carrots or sugar snap peas. My ultimate suggestion for this dressing is warming it over a low heat and whisking in cubes of cold butter until the sauce thickens to double (heavy) cream consistency, then pouring it over steamed white fish. Yellow bean sauce is available to buy from Asian supermarkets.

Makes 100ml (3½fl oz) VG

½ large bunch coriander stalks,
  roughly chopped
2 garlic cloves, sliced
5cm (2in) ginger, peeled and sliced
4 Tbsp yellow bean sauce
1 green chilli, sliced
20g (¾oz) palm sugar or dark
  brown sugar
1 Tbsp rice wine vinegar

Place all the ingredients into a small blender and blitz until smooth. It will store well in the fridge for up to 2 weeks.

Tamarind Dressing

Drawing inspiration from the wonderful tamarind dressings of India and Pakistan, this dressing is just perfect with fried battered things such as fish, chicken or even pastries. I find I crave a sour relief when I eat those rich items, and this tamarind dressing does just that.

Makes 250g (9oz) V

50g (1¾oz) tamarind pulp (p.40)
50g (1¾oz) caster (superfine) sugar
50g (1¾oz) honey
¼ tsp cayenne or chilli powder
a pinch of ground ginger
a pinch of cumin seeds, toasted and ground
6 turns black pepper from a mill

Prepare the tamarind pulp as on page 40.

Blitz all the ingredients together in a blender with 100ml (3½fl oz) water until smooth. Season with salt to taste. It will keep well in the fridge for 2–3 weeks.

Za'atar Dressing

Za'atar is a herb in its own right found throughout the Middle East. It is in the family of oregano – some people call it Syrian oregano – but the word is more commonly used to refer to za'atar, the spice mixture, which is seen in various incarnations throughout the Middle East and Levantine region. Typically, though, you'll find za'atar (the herb) alongside sesame seeds, dried sumac and salt. In this dressing, it has a wonderful fragrance. I use it in many ways, but one of my favourites is tossed through warm flat (romano) green beans. I prefer to use moscatel vinegar in this recipe but, to be honest, any vinegar will do (or even some lemon juice instead).

Makes 250g (9oz) VG

1 carrot, finely diced
1 celery stick, finely diced
1 onion, finely diced
150ml (5fl oz) extra-virgin olive oil
2 garlic cloves, finely grated
3 Tbsp vinegar (red, white, apple cider or moscatel)
3 Tbsp za'atar

Place the carrot, celery and onion in a pan, season with fine salt and cover with the olive oil. Over a gentle heat, simmer the vegetables for 15–20 minutes or until soft. Do not allow the vegetables to fry – they should cook with no colour. Add in the garlic and cook for a further 2 minutes. Take off the heat and add the vinegar and za'atar. The dressing will keep well in the fridge for up to 2 weeks.

PICKLES

Pickling Liquor

There are hundreds of ways to make pickles, but this is by far my favourite. It's mellow yet sharp. You can pickle almost anything, but my preferred veggies (other than red cabbage, which we make vat-loads of at our London restaurant) are cucumber, cauliflower and (bell) peppers. The pickles are ready to use within 2 days, but ideally leave for a week before using.

Makes 2L (70fl oz) VG

625ml (21 ½fl oz) apple cider
   vinegar
250g (9oz) caster (superfine) sugar
2 star anise
25g (1oz) allspice berries
30g (1 ¼oz) fine salt
500–600g (1lb 2oz–1lb 5oz)
   vegetables of your choice

Place 500ml (17fl oz) of the apple cider vinegar, the sugar, 1L (35fl oz) water, the spices and salt into a pan and gently bring up to the boil. Turn the heat off and leave the mix to stand for an hour.

Prepare your vegetables of choice by either slicing fine or cutting into small pieces and place into sterilized jars or containers with tight-fitting lids.

Bring the pickle liquor back up to the boil and add the remaining 125ml (4fl oz) vinegar. Strain off the spices and pour the hot liquid over the vegetables and place the lids straight on. It will keep for up to 6 months in a cool, dry and dark place unopened. Once open, store in the fridge and use within 4–5 weeks.

Pickled Turnips

This is a traditional way of pickling turnips in the Middle East, with the turnips turning a beautiful pink colour thanks to the beetroot and with a fabulous pungency from the garlic. You may wish to have a plate of them on the table if serving rich ragout, or chopped through a salad, or as part of a dinner to share.

Makes 1L (35fl oz) VG

500g (1lb 2oz) turnips, peeled
   and cut into batons
1 small red beetroot (beet), peeled
   and roughly chopped
1 garlic clove
125ml (4fl oz) distilled vinegar
330ml (11 ¼fl oz) şalgam (Turkish
   turnip juice, available from
   Middle Eastern supermarkets)
1 bay leaf
15g (½oz) fine salt

Place the turnips, beetroot (beet) and garlic into a sterilized jar. Bring 125ml (4fl oz) water, the vinegar, şalgam, bay leaf and salt up to the boil. Pour the hot liquor over the turnips, beetroot and garlic. Place a piece of baking paper directly over the turnips and put the lid straight on. Leave for a minimum of 2 weeks to pickle. It will keep for up to 6 months in a cool, dry and dark place unopened. Once open, store in the fridge and use within 4–5 weeks.

THREE RECI-PES

FRUIT

Sweet Melon & Pickled Peppers

Acid, texture and contrast can be deceptively simple. Find yourself the sweetest, softest melon. Pickle some peppers. Serve.
If you think about it (and I have), it has the three key building blocks in surplus.

It was actually my mum who gave me this tip on rapid pickling in malt vinegar (mums always know best). I like to add an extra level to this dish with a slight bitterness from the peppers, from the charring, which is even better done on a barbecue for smoky vibes.

Serves 4 VG

2–4 peppers of your choice
   (I like to use Turkish mild
   peppers)
malt vinegar (you can use other
   vinegars if you don't have any, but
   certainly don't use your finest)
1 sweet, ripe good-quality melon
   (any will do but cantaloupe
   works well)
sea salt flakes (kosher salt)

Heat the grill (broiler) to its highest setting. Place the peppers on a flat baking sheet and put under the grill to blister and blacken all over. Pop them into a bowl, cover and leave for 10 minutes. Rub off the blackened skins with your fingers and remove the seeds. Slice the peppers, season with fine salt and cover in malt vinegar. Leave for at least a few hours, although ideally overnight.

Cut the melon into wedges and remove the seeds. For each wedge of melon, cut the skin away and then place the flesh back onto the skin and cut each wedge into 4–6 pieces. Arrange the wedges on a plate, sprinkle over a pinch of sea salt flakes (kosher salt) and top with slices of pickled peppers.

Ideas & Inspirations

+ Try this with other naturally sweet and perfectly ripe fruit, such as peaches or pears.

+ Make this as part of a sharing feast. Definitely include some buffalo mozzarella, and muhammara (p.69), hummus (p.76), and chermoula beets, dates & pistachios (p.233) can join the party, too.

Apricot, Mint & Onion

Apricots and mint first made an appearance at my restaurant as a garnish for roasted pollock. The day I put it on the menu was also the day I had my old lecturers (from cooking college) in for their annual lunch. They are an absolutely lovely bunch of people and I have nothing but respect and love for them. They made sure the young, shy Selin I was back in the day was ready to face the big bad world of professional cheffing.

They are also classic stalwarts, and they will not hold back when it comes to (constructive) criticism and feedback. I thought perhaps apricots, raw onion and mint might be pushing the boat out a little bit too much. Several of them came by the pass after lunch to tell me how delicious the dish was, and how surprised they were by it. So, from my old lecturers to you, this will definitely pair well with a deliciously roasted piece of fish.

Serves 4 VG

4 apricots, perfectly ripe
¼ small onion, finely diced
½ tsp dried mint
1 tsp vinegar (red, white, apple cider or moscatel)
4 Tbsp extra-virgin olive oil
sea salt flakes (kosher salt)
8–10 small mint leaves

Halve the apricots, remove the stones and arrange the apricots on a plate.

Mix together the onion, dried mint, vinegar and olive oil. Season the apricot halves with sea salt flakes (kosher salt) and spoon over the dressing. Top with the mint leaves.

Golifa (Pomegranate, Wheat Berries, Almonds & Sultanas)

This is a very classic Cypriot dish. It is also incredibly hard to pin down what it is, exactly. It is a Turkish-Cypriot salad-muesli number which is both sweet and savoury and works well as a snack or as a dessert or as a side.

I grew up with its chameleon ways: once a year, when the pomegranates were in season, Mum would make bucketloads of it, and it would just be there in the fridge for us to snack on.

Serves 4–6 VG

125g (4½oz) wheat berries or
    pearl barley
100g (3½oz) skin-on almonds
2 pomegranates, seeds picked
100g (3½oz) sultanas
50g (1¾oz) sesame seeds,
    lightly toasted

The night before, soak the wheat berries in cold water, and pour boiling water over the almonds. Leave to soak.

Drain the wheat berries and place into a large pan, then cover with fresh, cold water. Bring up to the boil, then turn down to a gentle simmer. Cook according to packet instructions. Leave to cool completely once cooked.

Drain and peel the almonds, and then combine with the cooled wheat berries and the remaining ingredients. Best served a little chilled.

Black Figs, Feta & Red Wine

Black figs are one of my favourite fruits. I love them on their own, or in dishes like this paired with some salty cheese. Eating a fig will immediately transport me back to my grandparent's garden in Cyprus. They have a big old fig tree and, when I was a young girl, there was nothing better than sitting underneath its hand-like leaves eating fruit after fruit. I still get excited about fig season each year, and I will always plan in some dishes for our menus at the restaurant; this recipe, in several iterations, has featured more than once.

By no means do you need to go the full nine yards on this. If all you have time for is smashing a couple of figs over a piece of toast and then crumbling over some cheese, then do that.

Whatever route you do go down, please do not eat figs out of season. They are the absolute worst, and worse still because they are just so magical when they are properly ripe.

Serves 4 V

100ml (3½fl oz) red wine (full bodied)
40g (1½oz) dark brown sugar
1 small beetroot (beet) or ½ large beetroot, peeled and roughly chopped
1½ Tbsp vinegar (red, white, apple cider or moscatel)
6–8 black figs, perfectly ripe, cut into quarters
50–70g (2¾–3½oz) feta (I like to use sheep's milk feta)
5 chives, finely chopped
sea salt flakes (kosher salt)
extra-virgin olive oil

In a small pan, combine the red wine, sugar, beetroot (beet) and vinegar and place over a medium heat. Bring to a simmer and reduce for 10–15 minutes or until the mixture turns to a syrup-like consistency. A good way to test this (if you are unsure) is to put a little of the syrup, straight out of the pan, on a small plate. Place into the freezer for 5 minutes to cool it down. When you take it out and the syrup holds on the plate without running too quickly, then it's ready. If it completely sticks to the plate and doesn't run, then add a little water to the pan and adjust over a gentle heat.

Strain off the syrup (discard the beetroot) and leave to cool to room temperature.

To serve, coat the figs in the syrup. Arrange onto plates and then crumble over the feta. Sprinkle with chives, sea salt flakes (kosher salt) and a drizzle of your best extra-virgin olive oil.

Watermelon, Halloumi & Oregano

When I opened my first restaurant, Oklava, I knew for a fact I wanted to have some sort of grilled hellim (halloumi) on the menu. It is the national cheese of Cyprus, on both sides of the island, and it is a mandatory guest at all proper Turkish-Cypriot barbecues. At the restaurant, we grill it over coals and finish it off with olive oil, a squeeze of lemon, a drizzle of honey, and a sprinkle of dried oregano. The effect is magical: people really, really love it, and come back for it time and time again. I was surprised when I first noticed this effect; I guess I was taking halloumi for granted. But, when done right and grilled with care, it is really something special.

It pays to source good halloumi (there are some Greek and Turkish producers out there who are doing the real thing, with raw sheep's or goat's milk, in the UK) and use a barbecue if possible. Officially, halloumi can only be called halloumi if it's from Cyprus, so you may find it labelled somewhere as Cypriot-style cheese. The real secret is to cook it from room temperature, which gives you the best chance of achieving that marshmallow-like centre.

Serves 4 V

4 wedges watermelon
1 x 200–250g (7–9oz) block halloumi
extra-virgin olive oil
1 lemon, juiced
2–3 pinches of dried oregano
2 Tbsp honey (optional)

Slice the watermelon into 2cm (¾in) slices and arrange on a plate.

Heat up a large frying pan (skillet) over a medium heat. Cut the halloumi into 2cm (¾in) dice, then drizzle a little oil in the pan and add the halloumi. Cook for 1–2 minutes on each side, ensuring you allow the halloumi time to build a gorgeous golden brown crust. The pan may need a little extra oil as you turn the halloumi.

Scoop out the halloumi into a bowl. Dress with lemon juice, oregano, olive oil and the honey, if using. Scatter, while warm, over the sliced watermelon. Sprinkle with extra oregano.

Ideas & Inspirations

+ Cook the halloumi in the same way and garnish with either green tomato ketchup (p.72) and mint leaves; black olive dressing (p.79) and dukkah (p.44); muhammara (p.69) and spiced crumbs (p.47); or, for something a little more experimental, lemongrass caramel (p.65), cashew nut condiment (p.63) and coriander (cilantro) leaves.

Stone Fruits, Duck, Leeks & Miso

This is another one of those dishes that works well even when pared down all the way. Just the duck, fruits and miso dressing on their own will be delicious. But, if you have lots of time and are looking for a longer cook, then I suggest you go all the way and get yourself a whole duck.

Serves 4

4–6 Tbsp miso and lemon
    dressing (p.84)
4 duck legs
1 large or 2 small leeks, dark
    green tops cut off
4 Tbsp extra-virgin olive oil
25g (1oz) unsalted butter
1 garlic clove, bashed
1–2 red chillies, depending
    on how hot you like it
½ cucumber, cut in half lengthwise
    and seeds scraped out
2 Tbsp vinegar (red, white,
    apple cider or moscatel)
sea salt flakes (kosher salt)
6–8 stone fruits such as plums,
    peaches or nectarines,
    perfectly ripe
80g (2¾oz) white cabbage,
    finely sliced
1 red onion, finely sliced
1 big handful of coriander (cilantro)
    and mint, leaves picked

Heat the oven to 190°C/170°C fan/375°F/gas mark 5 and prepare the miso and lemon dressing as on page 84.

Season the duck legs with fine salt on both sides. Place, skin-side down, into a cold, ovenproof pan and place over a medium heat. Cook for 5–10 minutes, so that the fat starts to render out, then place into the oven and roast for 45 minutes. Turn the legs over so they are now skin side-up and continue to roast for another 45 minutes. Depending on how crispy you like your duck, you may wish to cook them for a little longer. Leave them to rest and cool a little.

Cut the leeks into 2cm (¾in) rounds. In a large, ovenproof frying pan (skillet) that will fit all the leeks, drizzle in 2 Tbsp of the olive oil and place over a medium–high heat. Add the leeks, standing up, cut-side down. Season with fine salt and cook for 3–4 minutes or until they start to turn dark brown. Add in the butter. Once it starts foaming at the edge of the pan, add in the garlic clove. Place into the oven and roast for 15–20 minutes or until the leeks are cooked through and tender.

Using a blowtorch or gas flame, blacken the outside of the chillies while holding them in tongs. If you have neither, you can also cook them under a hot grill (broiler), rotating regularly, until blackened and charred. Leave them to cool a little, then scrape some of the char off, but not all of it, as it provides good flavour.

Cut the cucumber into 1cm (½in) slices, place in a large bowl and coat in the vinegar and sea salt flakes (kosher salt). Remove the stones from the fruit and cut each half into 3–4 wedges. Add the wedges to the cucumber along with the cabbage, red onion, cooked leeks and herbs.

Break the warm duck into large pieces and place into the salad bowl. Drizzle over the remaining 2 Tbsp olive oil and season with sea salt flakes. Toss the salad gently together.

To serve, spoon generous amounts of miso dressing onto plates or a platter and top with the salad. Tear the chilli into strips and drape over to finish.

Ideas & Inspirations

+ Turn this dish into a feast by roasting a whole duck instead of just the legs. Roast for 2 hours at 180°C/160°C fan/350°F/gas mark 4, breast-side down. Flip halfway through, allow it to rest for 30 minutes and then rip into large chunks.

+ Duck loves fruit, so if stone fruits are not in season, use a fruit that is or even dried fruits. I particularly love dried sour cherries with duck.

+ Soak the sliced cabbage and red onion in iced water for 10 minutes to make them extra crisp.

ALL THINGS GREEN

Side Salad & Variations

A delicious side salad, made well and with love, is sometimes all you need to give a meal the acid, texture and contrast it needs. Take a piece of fish, meat or poultry (steamed, roasted or fried), add a salad with flavour, colours, excitement and anticipation (you may think I'm over the top, but I really believe the humble side salad can be all of those things), and an average meal becomes a stellar meal. It is the support act that sometimes can't help but steal the lead role.

A salad effortlessly marries my three building blocks: it will almost always contain acid from a good dressing, natural texture from vegetables, and contrast in flavour profiles and the different ways that ingredients feel and look. For me, it is the definition of moreishness and my dinner table is scarcely without one.

My 'recipe' for a side salad is more 'whatever the weather' rather than hard rules. I like to prepare a selection of ingredients, tub them up and fridge them. Then, I can use them throughout the week for quick, easy and very delicious lunches or dinners. My very own salad bar.

This idea was born out of necessity. I'm not one of those people that can 'pop' to the shop and just get three ingredients for dinner. Twenty minutes later and I'm back outside with two heavy bags of groceries, aching arms and still no clue what I'll cook that night. As a result, my fridge is almost always full, and the 'salad bar' was an easy way of processing my purchases: by cooking and preparing them, the ingredients could be shrunk into smaller containers. Turns out having a ready-made supply of ingredients is very convenient and allows more time for playing around with different combinations.

A Selin prep session involves a fair bit of steaming, roasting, and pre-dressing with olive oil and vinegar. Whole chickens get the chop: they'll be poached, and once they're cool I'll take the breasts off and marinate them in a soy sauce and garlic dressing. All my salad leaves and vegetables get a good wash (and hang out to dry on a dish towel while I potter about). Any sad-looking citruses get repurposed into dressings, of which I'll have a few ready-made to go. Stale bread finds new life as croutons. Nuts and seeds are roasted. It's not an exhaustive list, but you get the idea.

These are some of my favourite salad bar creations:

+ A wedge of iceberg lettuce (unfashionable, I know, but she's got some potential yet) can be very enticing with the addition of a creamy dressing. Take 4 heaped Tbsp of thick yoghurt and whisk in 2 Tbsp each of extra-virgin olive oil and lemon juice. Season the dressing with sea salt flakes (kosher salt) and smear all over a lettuce wedge. Get right in between those layers, too. Crumble or grate a cheese of your choice all over (I usually use feta and I'll keep a stock of it in the fridge) and grind lots of black pepper over the top. Finish with chopped chives or spring onions (scallions). To make it extra special you could put some crispy lamb bacon (p.212) or regular bacon over the top.

+ Chopped salad means just that: chop a bunch of ingredients up and dress them. I think the universal joy in a chopped salad is that each mouthful contains the entire salad, and that it therefore also contains all of the acid, texture and contrast in one go. There are endless varieties (literally, just take it and chop it) but one of my favourites is to blanch lots of green vegetables such as kale, broccoli, chard and turnip tops, squeeze all the excess water out of them, and chop up along with spring onions (scallions), plenty of herbs of your choice, and pears. Dice a block of halloumi and pan-fry in a little olive oil until golden brown and crisp. Add these to the bowl along with toasted seeds and nuts (p.49) and a sharp dressing with extra-virgin olive oil, vinegar and sea salt flakes (kosher salt). You could also add some cooked chickpeas (garbanzo beans), beans or lentils to this to make a meal in itself, and I usually can't resist a few pickled chillies in there, too.

+ Finely slice strips of sugar snap peas, carrots, red onion, cucumber and cabbage. Add lots of chopped coriander (cilantro), dress with palm sugar, chilli and lime dressing (p.83).

+ Slice varieties of bitter leaves, such as radicchio and chicory (endive), into random shapes and add orange or grapefruit segments. Coat in urfa chilli dressing (p.81) and top with toasted and chopped hazelnuts. A pool of thick yoghurt smeared under this salad is a very good thing, too.

+ Finely slice some cauliflower and add to a bowl of mixed greens such as romaine, kale, and salad leaves. Coat in a creamy tahini dressing – combine 2 Tbsp thick yoghurt, 3 Tbsp tahini, juice of 1 lemon, a pinch of sea salt flakes (kosher salt) and a splash of olive oil, with another splash of water if you think it's too thick. Top the salad with some crunchy textures from your salad bar – toasted seeds, dukkah (p.44) or croutons, for example.

+ Take a few big handfuls of mixed baby leaves and add some sliced apple and spring onions (scallions). Coat in a dressing made up of 1 Tbsp sesame oil, 1 Tbsp toasted sesame seeds, 1 tsp grated ginger, 1 Tbsp soy sauce, 1 tsp mirin, 1 tsp honey or sugar and 1½ Tbsp rice vinegar or lime juice – taste and adjust to your liking.

+ My last tip here is for a meaty dressing. Ingredients such as chorizo, pancetta, cured meats, cured fats (p.60) and chicken skin all contain oodles of flavour. Dice or slice one of these and slowly cook in a pan until they are golden, crisp and have leached out all their glorious oil. Add a little olive oil (maybe some garlic and thyme, too) and an acid of choice to the pan. Spoon this dressing warm over whatever you like – chunks of avocado or ripe peaches along with a handful of rocket (arugula). I would almost certainly get some croutons in there, too, to soak up all the dressing and for a bit of texture.

Gem, Dates, Crispy Lavash & Feta

I don't repeat many things I make but this salad I do. It's got sweetness from the dates, juicy crunchiness from the baby gem, a lovely fragrance from the herbs, and a dressing you throw together in an instant but which rewards you by smacking you around the face with flavour. Trust your own instincts and taste buds when dressing the salad and find what tastes good to you. Make it your own. I'll even forgive you if you pass it off as such.

Serves 4 V

8–10 crispy lavash shards (p.47)
6 Medjool dates, cut in half, pips removed
extra-virgin olive oil
200g (7oz) feta
2 baby gem, leaves separated
a big handful of picked herbs, such as coriander (cilantro), parsley, mint, chives or basil
vinegar (red, white, apple cider or moscatel)
sea salt flakes (kosher salt)

Prepare the crispy lavash shards as on page 47.

Cut each date half into 3 and place into a large bowl. Drizzle with olive oil and run them through your fingers so they separate out nicely. Crumble the feta into the dates, ensuring you keep some chunky pieces – you don't want it turning into a big mush by the time you've mixed it. Add the leaves and herbs to the bowl.

Now it's time to dress the salad and I would encourage you to freestyle this. As a general guideline, I like to do about 3 parts olive oil to 1 part acid. Following that rough measurement drizzle over the oil followed by your vinegar of choice, and season well with sea salt flakes (kosher salt). If you prefer you can measure the dressing into a bowl and taste it first. Give the salad a good mix (it really is best to get your hands in there). Taste to ensure there is enough salt, oil and acid, and adjust as necessary. A measure of a good dressing is if one bite isn't enough.

Add the crispy lavash and mix again, making sure you coat the shards with everything without breaking them up too much. Serve immediately

Ideas & Inspirations

+ You could replace the Medjool dates with dried or fresh fruit you like. My favourite variation is natural dried apricots, bitter rocket (arugula) and crumbled goat's cheese.

+ Replace the crispy lavash with croutons, nuts, toasted seeds, crispy chickpeas (garbanzo beans), dukkah (p.44) or puffed grains, which you can buy online or in health food shops.

Asparagus, Candied Bacon & Graceburn

Graceburn is a soft cow's cheese in oil, the creamier cousin of feta, if you will. If you can't source it locally, you can find it online or switch in a decent feta. If you do go for another cheese, use some good-quality olive oil at the end. If you're a chilli addict, like I am, be sure to sprinkle some dried chilli (red pepper) flakes or chopped fresh chilli over this number.

One non-negotiable part of this dish is serving it with bread. It would be blasphemy not to have something to soak up all that deliciousness with.

Serves 4

8 rashers smoked streaky bacon
4 Tbsp maple syrup
12 large asparagus spears, ends trimmed
125g (4½oz) Graceburn cheese
1 Tbsp balsamic vinegar

Heat the oven to 190°C/170°C fan/375°F/gas mark 5.

Line a large baking sheet with baking paper and lay out the bacon rashers with space in between each slice. Place into the oven and cook for 10 minutes or until the bacon starts to brown. Brush over half the maple syrup and place back into the oven to cook for a few more minutes, then turn the bacon over, brush with the remaining syrup and put back in the oven for 2 minutes or until the bacon is golden and caramelized. Take out of the oven and leave to cool.

Place a large pan of salted water on to boil. Add the asparagus spears and boil for 1–2 minutes or until the spears feel tender. Drain and leave to cool slightly.

To serve, place the asparagus onto a large plate, season and crumble over the Graceburn. Spoon over plenty of the oil from the cheese so it pools on the plate. Drizzle over the balsamic vinegar, before adding the bacon.

Ideas & Inspirations

+ You can use honey or treacle (molasses) instead of maple syrup.

+ Cook the asparagus spears and serve warm with slices of miso butter (p.70) to melt over.

+ Cook the asparagus spears, leave them to cool, and drizzle over some tamarind dressing (p.85) and cashew nut condiment (p.63).

Aegean Greens, Whipped Feta & Za'atar

Along the Aegean coast in Turkey people will often forage for greens and (what other people perceive as) weeds, boil them and serve them doused in lemon juice, garlic, olive oil and sometimes vinegar. Some common plants they'll encounter along the coast are wild asparagus, wild leek, black mustard and samphire.

It was Cretan migrants who originally brought this technique with them when they moved to the area, and foraging is a key part of the Mediterranean diet, pre-dating any modern fascination we might have with it. I love this about cooking and eating: it develops and changes as people and ideas and methods move around. Food is heavily reliant on freedom of movement and the intrinsic need of people to eat and share, wherever they go.

I wanted to recreate the freshness and greenness of this simple dish. This recipe would work really well as a sharing plate, with lots of bread for dipping in it, or a side for any dinner. The key is using greens that are super seasonal. Better yet, the next time someone hands you a bag of foraged greens, I suggest you give them the Aegean treatment.

Serves 4 V

400g (14oz) feta
5 Tbsp double (heavy) cream
800g (1lb 12oz) seasonal greens
    such as kale, puntarelle, spinach,
    spring greens, sprout tops, Swiss
    chard, turnip tops, etc.
80ml (2½fl oz) extra-virgin olive oil
1 garlic clove, finely chopped
1 Tbsp vinegar (red, white,
    apple cider or moscatel)
    or lemon juice
sea salt flakes (kosher salt)
25g (1oz) za'atar

Blitz the feta in a blender until smooth. Whip the cream to soft peaks and fold the feta into the cream.

Bring a large pan of salted water up to the boil. If some of the greens are big or particularly stalky, remove the chunky stalks and cut them all into roughly the same-sized pieces.

Cook the greens in the boiling water, in batches, for 3–4 minutes – extra time might be required for greens with tougher stalks. Drain and allow to cool slightly, ensuring they retain some heat. Mix together the olive oil, garlic and vinegar, add the greens and season to taste with sea salt flakes (kosher salt).

To serve, smear the whipped feta all over a plate, pile up the greens and sprinkle over the za'atar.

Ideas & Inspirations

+ The za'atar could be replaced with toasted sesame seeds and sumac, or try spiced crumbs (p.47), dukkah (p.44), or buttered crumbs and sour shallots (p.43).

+ If you're foraging yourself, look out for things such as nettles. Or 'forage' in your kitchen and chop off the top of beetroot (beet) leaves and spinach stalks.

Cucumber, Sorrel, Runner Beans & Green Tomatoes

There is some great natural acidity to be had in vegetables – green tomatoes and sorrel chief among them. They've got so much of their own that this recipe really doesn't need any extra vinegar or lemon, but if you're an acid addict like me, you might want to add a little extra anyway. You won't find these two particular ingredients in your average supermarket, so seek them out via good local markets and your friendly restaurant supplier.

Runner beans and green tomatoes are in season around the same time of year (late summer), along with different varieties of cucumbers. They all marry together perfectly. This dish would be delicious with fatty roast meat such as duck. If you find yourself with a bounty of green tomatoes I suggest you also make green tomato ketchup (p.72). It's a sweet and sour condiment and works with just about anything, even this salad.

Serves 4 VG

160g (5¾oz) runner (string) beans, strings removed
25g (1oz) sorrel
100ml (3½fl oz) neutral oil (grapeseed, preferably)
1 cucumber, peeled and seeds removed
2 green tomatoes
1 fennel, fronds reserved
sea salt flakes (kosher salt)

Bring a pot of salted water up to the boil. Cut each runner (string) bean on angle into 4 pieces. Boil the beans for 2–3 minutes or until just cooked. Drain and leave to cool.

Blitz together the sorrel and oil in a blender until smooth.

Slice the cucumber into random-sized chunks. Cut the tomatoes in half and slice each half as finely as you can.

Slice the fennel as finely as you can with a knife, or wafer-thin with a mandoline – please make sure not to slice your fingers. Put the fennel into iced water for 5 minutes to crisp up, then drain and dry off a little with a clean dish towel.

In a bowl, combine the cucumber, runner beans, tomatoes and fennel. Season with sea salt flakes (kosher salt) and dress with the sorrel oil. Scatter over any fennel fronds, to serve.

Trombetta Courgettes, Butter Beans & Spiced Mayo

I'll be honest, I'm not really a fan of regular courgettes (zucchini). This is a well-kept secret, as they are a Mediterranean staple and therefore make a regular appearance in a certain Turkish dish I cook.

However, I have to say I do enjoy these funky shaped trombetta courgettes: not only for their psychedelic shapes but also because they have much more flavour and are much firmer than the dark green varieties we are most used to.

Serves 4 V

2–4 Tbsp spiced mayo (p.75)
150g (5½oz) dried butter (lima) beans, soaked overnight and drained
1 carrot, cut into 4
1 onion, quartered
1 celery stick, cut into 4
2 bay leaves
2 trombetta courgettes (zucchini), cut into 2cm (¾in) chunks
80g (2¾oz) unsalted butter
½ lemon, juiced
1 big handful of flat-leaf parsley, chopped

Prepare the spiced mayo as on page 75.

Add the drained beans, carrot, onion, celery and bay leaves to a large pan and fill with enough water that it's 2–3cm (1in) above the beans. Place over a medium–high heat, and once the water comes up to the boil, turn the heat down to a gentle simmer and cook for 45 minutes–1 hour or until the beans are just cooked. Season the beans well with fine salt and add the courgettes (zucchini). Continue to cook for 20 minutes or until the courgettes are soft. The liquid should have reduced considerably and be barely covering the beans, but if there is more, drain the excess water, keeping around 2 ladles' worth.

Add the butter and stir to emulsify with the water. Finish with the lemon juice and parsley and check the seasoning for salt. Season with plenty of freshly ground black pepper and serve in bowls with a big dollop of spiced mayo on top.

Ideas & Inspirations

+ Courgettes (zucchini) are in season in the summer, but you could also try this with a marrow (in late summer and autumn) or fennel or pumpkin (in winter).

+ This could be a side, or the main event along with a side salad (p.104). Sprinkle over some buttered crumbs and sour shallots (p.43).

Greens & Fried Onion Condiment

This condiment takes inspiration from the dark, red and sticky sauces you will find in kitchens and cuisines around the world – XO, gochujang, harissa, hoisin, adobo, and more. We humans share a penchant for big flavours in small quantities – flavours that will provide a hit of umami, sweetness, and punchiness, and lift up the dish they are added to. We all eat differently, and these differences are wonderful, but it seems some forms of imparting flavours are hardwired into us as humans and will pop up in whichever part of the world you sit down to eat.

One of my favourite ingredients in Turkish cookery is sun-dried pepper paste, which you can get in a mild (tatli biber salçasi) or hot (aci biber salçasi) versions from Middle Eastern supermarkets. I love discovering ways to use it, and here it works perfectly to achieve a bowl of 'eat me'! I love it with simple seasonal greens, like this, but you can also have it with some poached or roasted chicken, swirled through thick yoghurt and topped with battered fried fish, or just spread over slices of a good loaf of bread.

Serves 4 VG

4–5 Tbsp crispy shallots
  (p.48, optional)
200–300g (7–10½oz) greens
  such as cabbage, kale,
  puntarelle, spring greens,
  sprouts, Swiss chard, turnip
  tops, Asian greens, etc.

For the fried onion condiment
150ml (5fl oz) neutral oil
  (grapeseed, preferably)
2 onions, diced
3 garlic cloves, finely sliced
160g (5¾oz) mild Turkish
  pepper paste (tatli biber salçasi)
1 tsp dried chilli (red pepper) flakes
  or powder (pul biber, preferably)
1 tsp sugar (dark brown, preferably)
2 tsp vinegar (red, white,
  apple cider or moscatel)

Prepare the crispy shallots as on page 48, if using.

To make the condiment, heat a large wide-based pan with the oil over a medium–high heat. Add in the onions and fry for 15–20 minutes or until the onions are a deep golden colour. Add the garlic and cook for 2 minutes. Add the pepper paste, chilli (red pepper) flakes and sugar and season with fine salt. Turn the heat down to low. Continue to cook for 10 minutes, stirring occasionally. Turn the heat off and add the vinegar. This condiment will keep well in the fridge for 3–4 weeks.

Bring a large pan of salted water up to the boil. Prepare your greens by chopping the leaves and thin stems into thick slices and thicker stems into small pieces. Add the thicker stems to the boiling water and cook for 2–3 minutes. When you think they may be ready, taste one to see if it is done to your liking. Add in the thinner, leafier green parts, which should only need a minute to wilt. Drain thoroughly. Smear the fried onion condiment on the plate and add the greens on top. Sprinkle with crispy shallots, if you like.

Cucumber, Yellow Bean & Crispy Shallots

This is so simple it's barely a recipe, which somehow makes it even more rewarding. It verges on being a relish or condiment and works well with the spice and flavour of dishes from South and Southeast Asia. Cucumbers can take all sorts of strong flavours and still shine through with their distinct juiciness.

My partner, bless her, is a bit of a sucker for carbs and claims she has a second stomach just for rice. This works perfectly as a garnish on top of a lovely bowl of just that (and at least allows her to enjoy something green along with all that rice), or you could toss this as a dressing through some cold noodles.

Serves 4 VG

2 Tbsp crispy shallots (p.48)
3–4 Tbsp yellow bean dressing
  (p.84)
1 cucumber, peeled
1 small handful of coriander
  (cilantro), leaves picked

Prepare the crispy shallots as on page 48 and the yellow bean dressing on page 84.

Cut the cucumber in half lengthwise. Using a teaspoon, scrape out all the seeds and then slice the cucumber into 1cm (½in) pieces. Season with fine salt and leave to sit in a colander for 30 minutes.

To serve, coat the cucumbers with the yellow bean dressing, place onto a plate and scatter with coriander (cilantro) leaves and crispy shallots.

NUTS

Grilled Seafood, Cashew Nut Condiment & Watermelon

There really is nothing better than preparing and sharing good food with the people you love. Even years of blood, sweat and tears in the professional kitchen have not managed to dull this ardent desire in me to feed others. I am completely in love with barbecuing and I will take any opportunity to grill meat, fish, or vegetables over hot coals. It's probably the Cypriot islander in me. But, if you are not in the mood to light a barbecue, you could coat the seafood here in flour or cornflour (cornstarch) and fry until crisp. Or, you could roast, poach, steam or grill (broil) them. Use whatever seafood you fancy or just one type – head to a fishmonger to see what they have. If you didn't want to make the lemongrass caramel, you could just use a little sugar to balance out the acidic lime and pungent fish sauce.

Serves 4

3–4 Tbsp lemongrass caramel (p.65)
3–4 Tbsp tamarind dressing (p.85)
4–5 Tbsp crispy shallots and
    crispy garlic (p.48)
125g (4½oz) cashew nut
    condiment (p.63)
2 squid, cleaned and gutted
2 large or 4 small fillets of mackerel,
    red mullet, salmon, sea bass, sea
    bream or trout
8 langoustines or prawns (shrimp),
    shell-on, intestinal tract removed,
    split in half
120g (4¼oz) beansprouts
500g (1lb 2oz) watermelon, seeds
    removed, cut into large dice
1 small handful each of mint and
    coriander (cilantro), leaves picked
1 small handful of basil leaves
    (Thai, preferably)
4 spring onions (scallions),
    finely sliced
1 lime, juiced
2 Tbsp fish sauce
1–2 chillies, finely chopped
sea salt flakes (kosher salt)
neutral oil

Prepare the lemongrass caramel (page 65), the tamarind dressing (page 85), the crispy shallots and garlic (page 48), and the cashew nut condiment (page 63).

Light the barbecue coals in a tower and burn for 45 minutes or until they turn a grey ash colour. Only disperse the coals once you are ready to use them, so they retain their heat. Place the grill bars on to heat up at least 10 minutes before use – the coals need to be very hot so ensure you time this correctly. Cut the squid down one side and open out like a book, then score the inside in a criss-cross fashion. Cut the squid into random triangular pieces. Cut any tentacles in half or into thirds if they are very big. Dry all the squid pieces thoroughly with paper towel. Dry the fish portions and langoustines (shrimp) in the same way.

Bring a pan of water up to the boil and drop in the beansprouts for 90 seconds. Drain and leave to cool on a tray.

In a large bowl, mix together the watermelon, beansprouts, herbs and spring onions (scallions). In a small bowl, whisk together the lemongrass caramel, lime juice and fish sauce. Add 1 or 2 chopped chillies, depending on how hot you like it. Add the dressing to the salad just before serving and season with sea salt flakes (kosher salt).

(continued overleaf...)

Coat the fish fillets and langoustines with just a little oil and season with fine salt. Season the squid with fine salt too but no oil.

Place the squid tentacles on the grill first and cook for 30 seconds before adding the triangular pieces of squid, which should be laid on the bars scored-side down. In total, the squid tentacles and pieces should take around 1–2 minutes, turning every 30 seconds or so. If you like your squid to have some charred edges, make sure your grill is nice and hot. But, it is better that the squid is cooked until tender, rather than overcooking it trying to get colour. Place the squid to one side while you cook the rest of the seafood. Reheat just before serving, if need be.

Place the fish fillets skin-side down onto the bars and leave for at least 2 minutes or until you see the skin beginning to caramelize. Using a thin metal spatula, lift a corner of the fish to check if it is ready to turn. Once flipped, depending on the size of the fillets, the fish should take 30–60 seconds to finish cooking. Leave to rest for 5 minutes – in this time the fish will continue to gently cook. Place the langoustines cut-side down and cook for 1–2 minutes on each side or until the shrimp turns white in colour and feels firmer.

Dress the salad, when you're ready to serve, and pile onto one side of a platter, then top with crispy shallots and garlic. Pile the seafood up on the other side and serve the tamarind dressing and cashew nut condiment on the side for sprinkling over everything.

Ideas & Inspirations

+ Grill the seafood as above and dress with the garlic, chilli, and sherry vinegar oil (p.56).

+ Dress the seafood with za'atar dressing (p.85) and serve with cucumber, sorrel, runner beans and green tomatoes (p.112) at a later summer barbecue. The rainbow of green colours in this combination is best served in the sunshine.

Raw Vegetables, Nut Butter & Vinaigrette

With this salad, it's really up to you to make it as exciting or simple as you want, and to use your choice of vegetables. As a general rule of thumb, if they are in season at the same time, vegetables will work well together on the plate. Try to find the best and most colourful vegetables you can, and why not try varieties you haven't used before? Your greengrocer can help you.

You can pretty much use any nut you like for the butter and vinaigrette, or even a mix. Make sure they are the best quality and raw. Some of my favourites are cashews, hazelnuts and pistachios. This amount of nut butter will make more than you need, but you achieve a better consistency if the machine has more to grind up. Keep the nut butter in a sterilized jar in the fridge for up to 4 weeks and use at breakfast time with toast, granola, pancakes or French toast.

Serves 4 V

400g (14oz) nuts, raw and peeled
sea salt flakes (kosher salt)
400g (14oz) mixed vegetables
   such as artichokes, beetroot
   (beets), carrots, celeriac (celery
   root), cucumber, firm tomatoes,
   puntarelle, radishes, spinach
   and sugar snap peas
1 big handful of mixed herbs
   such as coriander (cilantro),
   flat-leaf parsley and mint,
   leaves picked

For the nut vinaigrette
2 Tbsp nut oil such as walnut
   or hazelnut
2 Tbsp extra-virgin olive oil
1 Tbsp honey
1½ Tbsp vinegar (red, white,
   apple cider or moscatel)
2 Tbsp nuts, toasted and chopped
(reserved from the nut butter)
10 chives, finely chopped

Heat the oven to 190°C/170°C fan/375°F/gas mark 5.

Scatter the raw nuts onto a baking sheet and place into the oven to toast for 8–10 minutes, or until golden and fragrant. If the nuts have skins on them, place into a clean dish towel after roasting and rub together to remove as much of the skins as you can.

While the nuts are still warm, place into a blender and blitz until they resemble a crumb. Take out 2 Tbsp for the dressing. Continue blending and every minute or so stop the machine, scrape down the sides with a spatula and blitz again. You will need to blend the nuts for several minutes and eventually you will see a buttery texture form. Season with sea salt flakes (kosher salt).

Slice, dice and mandoline the vegetables into all sorts of shapes and sizes. Alternatively, you can use the slicing and grating attachments on a food processor – do what feels right for you.

Whisk together all the ingredients for the vinaigrette and season to taste with sea salt flakes.

To serve, smear a generous spoonful of nut butter down one side of a plate and then layer up with the vegetables and the herbs, ensuring you mix different colours and shapes to make it visually enticing. Season with sea salt flakes as you go and spoon over the dressing.

Alternatively, dress the vegetables with the nut dressing in a bowl and plate up. For an extra special touch, you can also finely grate a nut over the salad to create a snow effect.

Braised Radicchio, Quince, Molasses & Pistachios

If you happen to come across a funky-shaped sister or brother of radicchio – aka tardivo or treviso – then please do bring them home, as variety is the spice of life and they also tend to be a little meatier (which is great for braising). The bitterness of the leaves serves as a brilliant contrast to the sweet yet acidic quince.

The cheese and butter in the juices provide a mellow creaminess.

If you prefer, you could skip the braising of the radicchio and just use the molasses, olive oil and vinegar as a dressing for the leaves.

Serves 4 V

extra-virgin olive oil
1 head of radicchio, quartered
80ml (2½fl oz) molasses, such
   as date, grape or mulberry,
   plus extra to serve
1 Tbsp vinegar (red, white,
   apple cider or moscatel)
20g (¾oz) unsalted butter
1 small handful of mint,
   leaves picked
16 red grapes, cut in half
4 Tbsp pistachios, toasted
   and chopped
40g (1½oz) pecorino, parmesan
   or other hard cheese
sea salt flakes (kosher salt)

For the sweet pickled quince
100g (3½oz) caster (superfine)
   sugar
125ml (4fl oz) distilled white
   vinegar, apple cider vinegar,
   or white wine vinegar
1 large or 2 small quince

Heat the oven to 180°C/160°C fan/350°F/gas mark 4.

For the pickled quince, combine 375ml (13fl oz) water, the sugar and the vinegar in a small pot and bring up to the boil. Boil for 3 minutes. Meanwhile, peel the quince and cut into 6–8 wedges. Place the quince and the peelings into the pan and turn the heat to as low as it will go, covering the quince directly with a round piece of baking paper. Cook gently for at least 90 minutes or until the quince is soft. Use a skewer or tip of a small knife to check how soft it is. Once cooked, scoop out the quince and leave to cool. Reduce the liquor to a syrup, then discard the peelings. Once the quince has cooled, remove the core and cut into chunks. Place back into the warm syrup.

Place a large frying pan (skillet) over a high heat and add in a drizzle of olive oil. Add the radicchio quarters and sear on each side for 1–2 minutes or until a little charred, then transfer the radicchio to a baking pan. Whisk together the molasses, 1 Tbsp water and the vinegar with some fine salt and freshly ground black pepper. Pour the molasses mix over the radicchio and cover with foil. Place into the oven for 30 minutes, then remove the foil, baste the radicchio with the juices and bake for another 15–20 minutes. Remove the wedges and leave to cool a little. Whisk the butter into the remaining juices in the tray.

To serve, tear up the warm radicchio and arrange across a platter and spoon over the buttery juices. Drizzle with a little extra molasses, if you like. Arrange the pieces of quince with a little of their syrup in and around the radicchio, then scatter over the mint leaves, grapes and pistachios. Shave the cheese over using a peeler and finish with a drizzle of olive oil, sea salt flakes (kosher) and freshly ground black pepper.

Ideas & Inspirations

+ You could give your pistachios the salt
& pepper treatment (p.43), or replace them
altogether with the walnuts.

+ Alongside this recipe, make the gem,
dates, crispy lavash, & feta (p.106) and the
crispy fried aubergine, chilli sauce & garlic
yoghurt (p.157) for the most impressive of
vegetarian feasts.

Roasted Cauliflower, Tahini & Pecans

When roasted with lots of butter, cauliflower takes on an indulgent meatiness with lots of inherent nuttiness to it. It is no surprise it pairs so well with tahini and pecans. I love playing around with vegetables in this way, especially a vegetable, like cauliflower, that has had to endure a lot of overcooking and mushing over the years.

Use regular tahini if you can't find the black version (but the dramatic appearance of the black one is worth the effort of finding it).

Serves 4 V

2 large or 4 small cauliflowers
6–8 Tbsp natural cauliflower
  purée (p.52)
extra-virgin olive oil
150g (5½oz) unsalted butter
4–8 small cauliflower leaves
  (optional)
sea salt flakes (kosher salt)
4 Tbsp tahini (black, preferably)

For the dressing
80g (2¾oz) pecans, toasted
  and crushed
4 natural dried apricots,
  finely chopped
1 tsp thyme leaves, chopped
10 chives, finely sliced
1 Tbsp capers, rinsed and chopped
4–5 Tbsp extra-virgin olive oil
1 tsp maple syrup
1 Tbsp vinegar (red, white,
  apple cider or moscatel)

Heat the oven to 210°C/190°C fan/415°F/gas mark 6–7.

Cut 4 steaks from the central part of the cauliflowers – if the cauliflowers are large you should be able to cut 2 steaks from each. Alternatively, you could just cut wedges and follow the recipe as per normal. Use the leftover cauliflower to make the cauliflower purée (as per page 52).

Put a little olive oil in a large, ovenproof frying pan (skillet) and place over a medium–high heat. Add the steaks (you may need to do this in two separate pans) and sear for 1–2 minutes on each side or until golden brown. Season both sides with a little fine salt, turn the heat down and add in half the butter. As the butter melts, use a spoon to keep basting it over the cauliflower. Once you have basted the cauliflower a few times, add the remaining butter to the pan, turn the cauliflower over and place in the oven for 10–15 minutes. Baste the cauliflower halfway through the cooking time. Take the cauliflower out and drain on a piece of paper towel. Before serving, place the cauliflower leaves, if using, into the hot butter and baste for 20–30 seconds or until they turn golden brown. Drain on paper towel and season with fine salt.

Mix together all the ingredients for the dressing.

To serve, smear the cauliflower purée onto the plate, drizzle around the tahini, add the cauliflower steaks, spoon over the dressing, and cauliflower leaves (if using).

Ideas & Inspirations

+ You could also just coat the cauliflower florets in a little olive oil, season – a dusting of Kyseri spice (p.56) or curry powder would be fabulous, too – and bake at 210°C/190°C fan/415°F/ gas mark 6–7 for 15 minutes, or until soft with golden edges. Be careful tasting them, you may find it hard to stop.

+ Instead of making a purée, you could chop up the trim of the cauliflower, caramelize in some butter and, once cool, blend through some thick yoghurt, to provide a creamy contrast to the cauliflower steaks.

+ The cauliflower steaks would work really well with a nut butter and nut vinaigrette (p.122).

Recipes: Nuts

Prawns, Coconut Chutney & Green Chilli Jam

Prawns, coconut and chilli are a match made in heaven, and a lovely reminder of sunnier climates (especially when you live somewhere gloomy and cold). Even just coating the prawns in this spiced batter and serving with some mayonnaise (p.75) feels indulgent and warming.

If you do make the coconut chutney and green chilli jam, I reckon it pays to make a bigger batch so you have some extra sitting in the fridge. The chutney will keep happily for 3 weeks, the jam for up to 3 months. Spoon it onto all sorts, from crackers to curries to runny eggs in the morning – try this last one especially, and then mop up all that joy with some roti, paratha or chapati.

Serves 4

3–4 Tbsp green chilli jam (p.71)
120g (4¼oz) plain (all-purpose) flour, plus extra for dusting
½ tsp smoked paprika
½ tsp coriander seeds, toasted and ground
1 tsp fennel seeds, toasted and ground
1 tsp onion or nigella seeds
200ml (7fl oz) sparkling water
neutral oil, for deep frying
12–16 raw tiger prawns (shrimp), peeled and intestinal tract removed
12 curry leaves
1 small handful of coriander (cilantro), leaves picked
1 lime, cut into wedges

For the coconut chutney
1 Tbsp tamarind pulp (p.40)
150g (5½oz) desiccated coconut
50g (1¾oz) coconut flour
200ml (7fl oz) full-fat coconut milk
20g (¾oz) palm sugar or light brown sugar

Prepare the tamarind pulp (page 40) and the green chilli jam (page 71). Place all the ingredients for the coconut chutney in a small pan, along with 2 Tbsp water, and place over a low heat, whisking as it cooks, for 20–25 minutes or until golden brown and caramelized. Allow to cool.

Whisk together the flour, paprika, seeds and sparkling water to form a batter. Fill a large pan halfway up with neutral oil and place over a high heat. You want the oil to get to 180°C/350°F on a temperature probe, or it should sizzle immediately when you drop a cube of bread in the oil.

Season the prawns with fine salt and then dust in plain (all-purpose) flour. Drop the prawns into the batter and coat thoroughly. Carefully lower the prawns into the hot oil (making sure you lay them away from you to prevent painful splatters). Depending on the size of the pan, you may need to do this in 2 batches as it's important you don't overcrowd the pan. Fry for 2–3 minutes or until the batter is crisp and golden. Drain onto paper towel and season with a little extra fine salt.

Drop the curry leaves into the hot oil and fry for 10–15 seconds or until they turn a darker green colour. Drain on paper towel.

To serve, spoon some coconut chutney on the bottom of a plate and pile the prawns on top. Spoon some green chilli jam around and over the prawns and finish with the crispy curry leaves and coriander (cilantro) leaves. Serve with lime wedges.

Hot 'n' Sour Lychee, Cucumber & Peanuts

This recipe takes inspiration from a dish I had on the menu many years ago when I was a head chef at Kopapa. I was still young and relatively carefree and full of energy. Once in a blue moon I would happily go and dance the night away in Soho after work, and would be back behind the stove by the time the sun rose. I took those levels of energy for granted, and now I'm happy if I can make it home in one piece after a full day in the kitchen. This was also my first role as a head chef, and those were formative years, not just for getting used to the level of responsibility a role like that entails, but for getting to grips and playing around with ingredients when I had full creative licence to do so.

We served the precursor of this dish with pork belly, and I would recommend this pairing. The fattiness of the meat is a great contrast to the zingy and fragrant flavours in the salad and sauce. A slow-roast lamb or mutton shoulder would pair brilliantly, too. You can make your own, of course, but there are some brilliant curry pastes on the market these days. Ensure you hunt down a good one.

Serves 4 V

For the hot 'n' sour sauce
90g (3¼oz) palm or dark
   brown sugar
2 Tbsp Thai red curry paste
4 Tbsp Chinese black rice
   vinegar (chinkiang)
1 hot red chilli, split in half
4 Tbsp rice wine vinegar
1 x 400ml (14fl oz) can
   coconut milk
2 Tbsp soy sauce

For the salad
150g (5½oz) beansprouts
300g (10½oz) lychees, fresh
   or canned
1 cucumber, cut in half, seeds
   scraped out, and cut into
   1cm (½in) slices
1 big handful of mint and coriander
   (cilantro), leaves picked
40g (1½oz) peanuts, toasted
   and roughly chopped
1–2 chillies, finely sliced (optional)
2 limes, juiced

To make the sauce, add the sugar to a wide-based pan over a low heat and gently cook the sugar to a caramel. Add the curry paste and cook for a further 2 minutes. Add 120ml (4fl oz) water, the chinkiang vinegar, chilli and rice wine vinegar, turn up the heat and boil for 10 minutes. Take off the heat and leave to infuse for at least 1 hour, or ideally overnight.

Strain the liquid and return to the pan. Add the coconut milk and bring back up to the boil. Turn down to a simmer and cook for 5–8 minutes or until thickened. Add the soy sauce and leave to cool to room temperature.

Place a pan of salted water on to boil. Cook the beansprouts for 90 seconds, drain and allow to cool on a baking sheet. Combine with the remaining salad ingredients in a bowl and season with sea salt flakes (kosher salt).

To serve, pool the sauce into the bottom of a bowl and top with a big pile of the salad.

SEA FOOD

Avocado, Brown Shrimp, Candied Lemon & Spiced Crumbs

Avocados are seemingly everyone's best friend. For me, they are a bit love or hate – any ingredient I see too much of, I start resenting just a tad (except maybe lamb bacon, you could wake me up for that any time of day). Having said that, avocados do have their merits and they lend themselves well to big flavours.

When picking an avocado, gently squeeze the top to see if it gives way; this is an indication it's ripe. Avocados respond well (flavour-wise) to a big hit of acid, and it will also help to stop them browning quickly once cut open. The spiced crumbs (p.47) really do add a lovely fragrance to this, so I would definitely push the boat out and make those.

Serves 4

2 Tbsp candied lemon (p.68)
3–4 Tbsp spiced crumbs (p.47)
2 large avocados
sea salt flakes (kosher salt)
5 chives, finely sliced
2 Tbsp extra-virgin olive oil
40g (1½oz) unsalted butter
70g (2½oz) brown shrimp

Prepare the candied lemon on page 68 and the spiced crumbs on page 47.

Open the avocados and remove the stones. While still in the skin, cut into slices, then run a spoon around the skin and remove the slices in one go. Place onto a serving plate and season with sea salt flakes (kosher salt).

Add the chives and the oil to the candied lemon.

Melt the butter in a small pan, add the shrimp, gently warm through for a minute or so and season with sea salt flakes

Spoon the warm shrimp over the avocados, followed by the candied lemon and a scattering of spiced crumbs.

Ideas & Inspirations

+ Instead of brown shrimp, you could use some smoked mackerel or smoked salmon. Dice them up and warm through in the same way.

+ I like using the candied lemon here for the sweetness it provides but, if you prefer, you could dice the skin of preserved lemon and mix through some olive oil, with a little squeeze of lemon juice as the dressing.

Sardine Escabeche, Rhubarb & Celery

Escabeche is one of those techniques that is known the world over. Technically, it refers to meat or fish that has been cooked and then marinated in an acid like vinegar or citrus fruit juice. It is very common in Spain, Portugal and Latin America, but it seems the original technique might have made its way there from Arabic and Persian cuisines in the 8th century. Seven centuries later and escabeche boarded the colonial ships of the Spanish and spread globally to regions under Spain's colonial rule – the Philippines, among others, does a mean escabeche which has been adapted to local ingredients.

Food never sits still, and it seems that despite the ravages of war and colonialism, cooking techniques have the power to far outlast the lives and times of their origins. It is worth finding out how something has landed on our plates, where it came from, and where it may go.

This dish is my contribution to the history of escabeche. Rhubarb is very sour when untreated with the tons of sugar we usually throw at it, and here it is a perfect match for the oily fish.

Serves 4

1 onion, finely sliced
3 garlic cloves, finely sliced
2 carrots, peeled and finely sliced
2 celery sticks, peeled and
   finely sliced
2 rhubarb stalks, finely sliced
2 bay leaves
4 thyme sprigs
300ml (10½fl oz) extra-virgin
   olive oil, plus extra for frying
3½ Tbsp vinegar (red, white,
   apple cider or moscatel)
8 sardines, butterflied

Put the vegetables, herbs and olive oil in a large pan and season with a little fine salt. Bring the pan up to a simmer and cook for 5–10 minutes or until the vegetables are just tender. Take off the heat and add the vinegar. Cool to room temperature.

Season the sardines with fine salt on either side. In a large frying pan (skillet), over a high heat, cook the sardines in a little olive oil for 20 seconds or so on either side. Place onto a deep tray that will fit them in a single layer and pour over the marinade. Leave to marinate overnight before serving at room temperature.

Marinated Mackerel, Chicory & New Potatoes

I like big meals as much as the next person but sometimes you just want something satisfying on a humbler level: some crunchiness, the herbaceousness of a herb or two, a beautifully balanced hit of flavour. This is that dish, and it's perfect for a light lunch. Here, the bitterness of the chicory (endive) provides a lovely contrast to the honey and shallot dressing and the mackerel can shine and sing

Serves 4

3 Tbsp honey and shallot
  dressing (p.82)
4–8 marinated mackerel
  fillets (p.59)
400g (14oz) new potatoes
sea salt flakes (kosher salt)
2 heads chicory (endive),
  red and yellow
1 big handful of herbs such
  as coriander (cilantro), flat-leaf
  parsley, mint, and tarragon,
  leaves picked
10 chives, finely sliced

Prepare the honey and shallot dressing (page 82) and the marinated mackerel (page 59).

Place the new potatoes in a pan, cover with cold water and season generously with fine salt. Place over a high heat and bring to the boil. Turn the heat down to a simmer and cook for 15–20 minutes or until the potatoes are cooked through and soft. Drain the potatoes and leave to cool until just warm. Crush each potato a little, season with sea salt flakes (kosher salt) and coat in the honey dressing.

Cut the chicory (endive) into random shapes and add to the potatoes along with the picked herbs. Plate up the potatoes, top with the marinated mackerel and a little of the dressing from the mackerel. Sprinkle with the chives, to serve.

Ideas & Inspirations

+ You could make this even easier by buying some good-quality cured or smoked fish.

+ I love the slight bitterness of chicory (endive) here, but any salad leaves would work including gem, radicchio, rocket (arugula) and frisée.

+ For something a little creamier, instead of the honey and shallot dressing, try one of the potato salads (p.226).

Octopus, Spiced Aubergine & Grapes

Octopus might seem like a slightly daunting process but I will lift the curtain here and show you that it really isn't all that difficult.

Firstly, buy a frozen octopus. Don't bother getting to grips with a fresh one and even if you're sitting on a boat and have just fished it out of the waves yourself, I would still recommend freezing your catch.

Freezing and then defrosting octopus tenderizes the meat enormously and means you won't need to cook it for 3 days for it to still be like a shoe. Secondly, undercooking octopus is awful but overcooking it a bit really isn't as bad. It is a pretty robust seafood and can take a bit of overcooking. Check to see if it's cooked by cutting a bit off and tasting it – if it's chewy, you just cook it for longer. You can't really go wrong.

Serves 4

1 onion, quartered

1 bay leaf

2 star anise

1 x 1–2kg (2lb 4oz–4lb 8oz) frozen octopus, defrosted

24 red or green grapes, cut in half

1 celery stick, finely sliced

1 small handful of mint leaves

1 big handful of coriander (cilantro), leaves picked

sea salt flakes (kosher salt)

vinegar (red, white, apple cider or moscatel)

extra-virgin olive oil

For the spiced aubergine

2 Tbsp Kyseri spice mix (p.56), plus extra to serve

100ml (3¾fl oz) extra-virgin olive oil

2 banana shallots, cut into 1cm (½in) slices

2 aubergines (eggplants), cut into 2cm (¾in) chunks

125ml (4fl oz) red wine

1 large beetroot (beet), peeled and grated

Heat the oven to 190°C/170°C fan/375°F/gas mark 5 and prepare the Kyseri spice mix as on page 56.

To cook the aubergine, place a Dutch oven, with a lid, over a high heat. Add the olive oil along with the shallots and aubergine and fry for 2–3 minutes. Add the spice mix and cook for another minute. Add in the red wine, beetroot (beet) and season with fine salt. Place a lid on the pan and put in the oven for 1 hour. After the hour, remove the lid, stir and return to the oven with the lid off for 20–30 minutes or until the mix is a little caramelized on top. Keep warm.

Place a large pan of water over a medium–high heat along with the onion, bay leaf and star anise. Once boiling, dunk the octopus in the water 3 times, then place in the water head-side down. Bring the pan back up to the boil and then turn down to a simmer and cook for 30–40 minutes. To check the octopus is cooked, insert a skewer into the thickest part of the tentacles, it should go in and out without much resistance.

Leave the octopus to cool slightly and then cut each tentacle into slices. There is some meat around the head which is usable too, normally, so cut a little off and have a taste to see if you like it. The innards are inedible, so discard those.

In a bowl, combine the grapes, celery and herbs. Dress with sea salt flakes (kosher salt), vinegar and olive oil to your taste.

Serve the sliced octopus and salad with the spiced aubergine, and drizzle with a little oil and a dusting of the spice mix.

Ideas & Inspirations

+ The spiced aubergine is good tossed through some pasta, finished with a bit of basil. It also works really well alongside a slow-roast shoulder of lamb.

Squid, Korean Lettuce, Lardo & Corn

I came across a recipe for Korean lettuce (sangchu geotjeori) a while back and have been obsessed with it ever since. It is a very simply tossed salad with notes of vinegar, chilli and sweetness, often served next to grilled meats. I imagine it is a bit like the Korean version of the Cypriot chopped salad I grew up eating alongside grilled lamb chops. It's safe to say it is right up my alley.

You can char the squid in a frying pan (skillet) but perhaps a barbecue grill would be even more appropriate.

Serves 4

2 large or 4 small squid,
    cleaned and ink sacs removed
1 head of lettuce such as
    butterhead, iceberg or romaine
sea salt flakes (kosher salt)
2 Tbsp neutral oil
2 corn cobs, kernels sliced off,
    or 1 x 260g (9¼oz) can
    sweetcorn, drained
20g (¾oz) coriander (cilantro),
    leaves picked and stalks sliced
4 slices lardo

For the dressing
1 tsp fish sauce
1½ Tbsp soy sauce
1 tsp dark brown sugar
1 Tbsp rice vinegar
1 Tbsp sesame oil
1–2 Tbsp dried chilli (red pepper)
    flakes (Korean, preferably)
2 tsp sesame seeds, toasted
½ onion, finely sliced
1 garlic clove, finely grated
2 spring onions (scallions),
    finely sliced

Cut the squid down one side and open out like a book. Scrape away and discard any membrane on either side. Score the squid in a criss-cross pattern on the inside, then cut the squid into triangular shapes, all roughly the same size (see pictures). If you have the tentacles, cut these into 2–3 pieces.

In a large bowl, mix together all the ingredients for the salad dressing. Add the lettuce and season with some sea salt flakes (kosher salt). Massage the dressing, using your hands, onto the lettuce leaves and divide up onto 4 plates.

Heat a large frying pan (skillet) over a high heat until very hot. Add the oil, followed by the squid. Season with salt and ensure the squid is spread out over the surface of the pan. Leave the squid to go golden brown and char a little on one side. Once coloured, add in the corn and toss around for another minute. Take off the heat and add the coriander (cilantro) stalks.

Pile the squid and corn on plates next to the salad, top with the slices of lardo and a sprinkling of coriander leaves.

Ideas & Inspirations

+ Lardo is cured pork fat and very delicious. Buy it ready-sliced online or from a deli and just drape it over a piece of toast rubbed with garlic and then a little drizzle of olive oil. Heaven.

Pickled Shellfish, Greens & Grain Mustard

Treating raw greens with a good massage of acid and then plying them with mayonnaise will transform them into a nest of silky and crisp textures, which are an absolute joy with soft pickled shellfish. Fear not if you have made too much: it's really nice to have some of this shellfish left over in the fridge for a tasty nibble at a later date. Eat with crusty bread.

Serves 4

2–3 Tbsp mayonnaise (p.75)
1½kg (3lb 5oz) mix of mussels, clams and cockles (or just one of them), rinsed thoroughly
250ml (9fl oz) extra-virgin olive oil
1 celery stick, finely sliced
1 carrot, split in half and finely sliced
1 onion, finely sliced
250ml (9fl oz) vinegar (red, white, apple cider or moscatel)
2 Tbsp caster (superfine) sugar
4 garlic cloves, finely sliced
1 chilli, finely sliced
2 Tbsp wholegrain mustard
500g (1lb 2oz) greens such as cabbage, kale, spring greens, sprouts or spinach
sea salt flakes (kosher salt)
½ lemon, juiced

Prepare the mayonnaise as on page 75.

Place a large, lidded pan, big enough to fit all the shellfish (or one that you can do in two batches) over a high heat. Add in the shellfish, along with a tiny splash of water and place a lid straight on. Cook for 2–3 minutes or until all the shells have opened up. Drain the shellfish and spread out over a large baking sheet so they cool rapidly. Remove the meat from the shells and place into a container that allows them to sit in one layer.

In a wide-based pan, heat half the olive oil over a high heat. Add the celery, carrot and onion and season with a little salt. Cook for 5 minutes or until the vegetables have softened slightly. Add the vinegar and sugar, turn the heat off immediately and pour over the shellfish.

In another small pan, heat the rest of the olive oil over a high heat and add the garlic and chilli. Cook until the garlic edges start to turn brown, take off the heat and add to the shellfish. Mix everything together thoroughly and leave to cool. Once cool, cover and place in the fridge and leave to marinate for at least 2 hours or preferably overnight.

Mix the mustard into the mayonnaise.

Finely shred or tear the greens into small pieces. Season with sea salt flakes (kosher salt) and squeeze over the lemon juice. Using your hands, massage the greens with the lemon. Mix in the mayonnaise.

Place a pile of the greens onto a plate, and top with the shellfish and vegetables.

Brown Crab, Sesame Noodles & Ponzu

My partner and I went to Norfolk for a holiday and, while there, she became slightly obsessed with the local crab fishermen. In Cromer, they launch their boats straight from the beach by backing them into the water on trailers pulled by a collection of the oldest, most beat-up, and most charming-looking tractors. We went to the beach to see them return at around 9 o'clock in the morning, when they approach the beach at full speed and launch themselves upon the pebbles. Many of these fishermen and their families have been fishing for Cromer crabs for generations. I say this because there are very good crabs to be had from UK waters, and I would encourage you to find them.

Not many people attempt cooking and picking a crab at home (it is a lot of work), and there are cooked and picked versions out there for sale. Although I would still recommend you pick through the meat to ensure there are no little pieces of shell. The best way to do this is to place all the crabmeat on one side on a flat baking sheet. Take little bits of the meat and gently pull it towards you with your fingers, checking for bits of shell and moving to one side of the tray if clear.

Bottled yuzu juice, dashi and kombu are available to buy in Japanese supermarkets and online, and you can buy ready-made ponzu these days, if you are short on time.

Serves 2

200g (7oz) soba noodles
1 Tbsp sesame oil, plus extra
    for coating the noodles
3 Tbsp sesame seeds, toasted
40g (1½oz) unsalted butter
2 Tbsp soy sauce
100g (3½oz) brown crabmeat
1 small handful of coriander
    (cilantro), leaves picked
2 spring onions (scallions),
    finely sliced

For the ponzu
2 Tbsp yuzu juice (or use a
    combination of lemon and lime)
4 Tbsp rice wine vinegar
4 Tbsp soy sauce
2 Tbsp sake
2 Tbsp mirin
2 Tbsp dashi

Cook the noodles according to packet instructions. Once cooked, rinse under cold water and drain thoroughly. Toss the sesame oil through the noodles.

Mix together all of the ingredients for the ponzu, along with 4 Tbsp water and 2 Tbsp of the sesame seeds.

Add the butter, the 1 Tbsp sesame oil and the soy sauce to a large frying pan (skillet) or wok and gently heat through. Once melted, add the brown crabmeat and mix thoroughly to break up all the crab. Take off the heat and toss through the noodles.

To serve, pile the noodles up high in a bowl and pour some of the ponzu around the noodles until it just pools on the bottom. Top with the coriander (cilantro), spring onions (scallions), and remaining 1 Tbsp sesame seeds.

NIGHTSHADES & MUSHROOMS

Tomato Salad & Variations

A good tomato salad is all about the tomatoes. This may come as no surprise, but it does bear repeating. Because of their incredible versatility (and because they are such a good vehicle for so many different flavours), we seem to want to eat them all year round. Often, this leads us to buy certain tomatoes in the wrong season, or to settle for the subpar quality of a tomato grown under glass.

The good news is that there are various types of tomatoes (not grown under glass) that are available in virtually every season of the year. The only thing you need to do is find the right place to source them from. One of my

suppliers at the restaurant (the mighty Natoora, who also supply homes) are known for their radical seasonality, and they have an amazing winter tomato. It's firmer and a little more acidic than a ripe summer tomato, and I absolutely adore them. It pays to source good produce.

Top-quality oil or fat and a good acid are also essential, but I could write a whole book dedicated to the ways to dress, eat and use tomatoes. If these recipes seem too time-consuming, you can always just create your own version. Acid, texture and contrast are (of course) key.

My Suggestions:

+ Dress tomatoes in olive oil, vinegar (your choice) and sea salt flakes (kosher salt) and top with croutons cooked in beef fat, beef scratchings (p.152), za'atar and a good kick of onion flavour in the form of chives or shallots.

+ Spoon a generous helping of muhammara onto a plate (p.69), top with diced tomatoes and finish with pomegranate dressing (p.82) and lots of shredded flat-leaf parsley.

+ Coat chunks of tomatoes in fried onion condiment (p.115) and top with crispy shallots and crispy garlic (p.48)

+ Cut tomatoes into small chunks, add lots of chopped coriander (cilantro), palm sugar, chilli and lime dressing (p.83), and top with crispy chickpeas (p.44) or pork crackling (p.219).

+ Caress tomatoes with chermoula (p.233), crumble over feta, and top with pitta croutons (p.46).

+ Slice a selection of tomatoes, arrange on a plate and top with sea salt flakes (kosher salt), lots of extra-virgin olive oil and a few drops of vinegar. Drizzle with sherry caramel (p.64) and top with spiced crumbs (p.47), chopped chives and lemon zest.

+ Cut large rounds of tomato and dress with lemongrass caramel (p.65), top with dried shrimp and citrus peel sambal (p.66) and shredded coriander (cilantro).

Aubergine, Lentil & Chipotle

This is a very flexible assembly of ingredients that could be eaten with a salad, tacos, eggs or roast chicken. You can use cooked lentils to make your life easier, and if you can't find canned chipotle, then replace with dried chillies and smoked paprika.

Serves 4 VG

125g (4½oz) Puy lentils, rinsed
2 aubergines (eggplants), diced into 2cm (¾in) cubes
2 Tbsp extra-virgin olive oil
2 banana shallots, finely sliced
2 garlic cloves, finely sliced
60g (2¼oz) canned chipotle chillies, roughly chopped (or 1–2 dried chillies if you can't find them)
½ cucumber, peeled into ribbons
1 small handful of coriander (cilantro), leaves picked
8 small romaine lettuce leaves
1 lime, zested and juiced

Heat the oven to 220°C/200°C fan/425°F/gas mark 7.

Place the lentils into cold water and bring up to the boil. Turn the heat down to simmer and cook for 20 minutes or until just cooked – they should be soft but still have some bite. Drain and leave to one side.

Place the aubergine (eggplant) in a roasting tin and drizzle over 1 Tbsp of the olive oil, along with a little fine salt. Place into the oven, stirring once halfway through cooking, for 20 minutes or until the aubergine is golden brown.

Place a pan on a medium heat, add the shallots and the remaining 1 Tbsp olive oil and cook for 10–15 minutes until soft and translucent. Add in the garlic and cook for a further 2–3 minutes. Remove from the heat.

Add the chillies to the shallots and garlic, then mix in the aubergines and lentils. Toss the aubergine mix with the cucumber, coriander (cilantro), lettuce leaves and the lime juice and zest, and season to taste. Add a little extra olive oil if you feel the mix is too acidic for your taste.

Ideas & Inspirations

+ Add more texture to this recipe with some toasted, crushed peanuts over the top.

+ Serve this with some crispy prawns (p.200), topped with coriander (cilantro) leaves, sliced spring onions (scallions), and lime wedges.

Steamed Aubergines, Beef Scratchings & Chilli Dressing

Lardo, Italian cured pig fat, has been having its moment for quite a while now. I absolutely love it, and it works so well thinly sliced on hot toast or on a dish as a sort of melt-in-your-mouth seasoning. I decided the magic curing process used for lardo should not be reserved just for the pig, but should be freely shared with the rest of the animal kingdom. Turns out curing the beef and lamb fat works equally well.

Another iteration is the very addictive beef scratchings in this recipe – best served warm or room temperature on toast so all the juices, combined with the fat from the scratchings, soak into the bread. Instead of aubergines (eggplants) you could use other vegetables, such as broccoli, courgettes (zucchini), asparagus, or green or runner (string) beans. Try to find different varieties of aubergines; I like to use baby ones when in season.

Serves 4

4–6 Tbsp chilli dressing (p.81)

100g (3½oz) cured beef fat (p.60)

2 large or 12 baby aubergines (eggplants)

60g (2¼oz) kale, stalks removed and leaves torn into small pieces

½ lemon, juiced

1 small handful of coriander (cilantro), leaves picked

2 spring onions (scallions), sliced

Heat the oven to 190°C/170°C fan/375°F/gas mark 5. Prepare the chilli dressing (page 81) and the cured beef fat (page 60). Dice the cured beef fat into small pieces, scatter across a baking sheet in 1 layer and place into the oven, stirring every 10 minutes or so, for 30 minutes or until golden brown and crisp. Drain off the excess fat but keep a little around the scratchings. Keep warm.

Bring a pan of water to the boil. If you are using baby aubergines (eggplants) then just prick them with the tip of a little knife all around; if you're using larger varieties, then cut them in half or quarters. Place the aubergines into a steamer cut-side up and steam for 15 minutes or until soft but not falling apart. You can check them by inserting your knife into the thickest part – if it comes out easily, they are ready.

Once the aubergine is cool enough to handle, peel off some of the skin. While they're still warm, coat them in 100ml (3½fl oz) of the chilli dressing and leave to one side.

Place the kale in a bowl, season with a little salt and pour over the lemon juice. Massage the kale to soften the texture a little.

Plate the aubergines, and scatter over the kale leaves, coriander (cilantro) and spring onions (scallions). Drizzle over the chilli dressing and a touch of salt. Scatter over the beef scratchings.

Soy-Pickled Mushrooms, Udon & Black Garlic

The liquid from these pickled mushrooms is so delicious. With added butter, it approaches sainthood. Some of my favourite mushrooms to use for this are hen of the woods, shiitake or king oyster. Feel free to use one type or many types. If you prefer, you could just finely chop some black garlic and toss through the noodles instead of making the purée.

Serves 4 V

200g (7oz) black garlic purée (p.51)
250g (9oz) udon noodles
125g (4½oz) unsalted butter, chilled and diced
4 spring onions (scallions), finely sliced

For the pickled mushrooms
500g (1lb 2oz) wild mushrooms
125ml (4fl oz) soy sauce
4 Tbsp vinegar (red, white, apple cider or moscatel)
60g (2¼oz) dark brown sugar
2 garlic cloves, bashed
3 thyme sprigs
neutral oil

Prepare the black garlic purée as on page 51.

Check through the mushrooms to ensure they are clean: use a brush or small knife to wipe away any dirt. If you think you may need to wash your mushrooms, do so, but ensure they are very dry before cooking. Cut or tear the mushrooms so they are roughly all the same size.

In a small pan, mix together the soy sauce, vinegar, brown sugar, garlic and thyme. Quickly bring to the boil, then immediately take off the heat.

Heat a large frying pan (skillet) over a high heat and add in a little neutral oil. Add in some of the mushrooms, ensuring they don't overlap, and the pan isn't overcrowded. Sear the mushrooms for 1–2 minutes or until there is a golden char on one side only. Take the mushrooms out of the pan and place into a container. Add a little more oil to the pan and repeat this process, using up all the mushrooms. Pour the hot pickle liquid over the mushrooms and leave for at least 4 hours or, preferably, overnight.

Cook the noodles according to packet instructions.

Strain the pickle liquid from the mushrooms into a large pan and place over a medium–high heat. Once the liquid is boiling, add 2–3 pieces of cold butter at a time and whisk to emulsify. Once all the butter is incorporated, turn the heat off and add the noodles, coating thoroughly in the sauce.

Pile the noodles in the centre of a bowl, top with the mushrooms, dots of black garlic purée and the spring onions (scallions).

Wild Mushrooms, Barley, Butterhead & Berkswell

This recipe plays with contrasting temperatures. The barley should be just warm, and this will work a dream with the cool salad.

If you can't get hold of Berkswell, use any semi-hard cheese.

Serves 4 V

4–6 Tbsp honey and shallot dressing (p.82)

extra-virgin olive oil

300g (10½oz) mixed wild mushrooms, torn or cut into 2–3cm (1in) pieces

30g (1oz) unsalted butter

2 banana shallots, finely diced

2 garlic cloves, finely grated

20g (¾oz) dried wild mushrooms, soaked in warm water and drained

150g (5½oz) pearl barley, thoroughly rinsed

1L (35fl oz) water or chicken or vegetable stock

1 butterhead lettuce, torn into pieces

1 small handful of herbs such as flat-leaf parsley, tarragon and chives

80g (2¾oz) Berkswell cheese, grated

Prepare the honey and shallot dressing as on page 82.

Heat a large frying pan (skillet) over a high heat and add a drizzle of olive oil. Add the wild mushrooms and cook for 2–3 minutes or until they have a little colour. Remove from the pan and leave to one side.

In a pan with a tight-fitting lid, melt the butter and another drizzle of olive oil over a medium heat. Add the shallots, with a little salt, and sweat with a lid on for 10 minutes or until soft. Add the garlic and cook for another 1–2 minutes with the lid off. Add the soaked and sautéed mushrooms followed by the barley and mix everything together until thoroughly coated in the butter. Add the water or stock and another pinch of salt. Place the lid on, stirring occasionally, and cook for 30–40 minutes or until the barley is just cooked. Allow to cool until just warm.

In a small bowl, mix together the lettuce with the herbs and coat with the honey dressing. Season with salt and freshly ground black pepper.

Serve the cooled barley in bowls and top with the salad and plenty of grated cheese.

Ideas & Inspirations

+ Instead of the honey and shallot dressing, a good tahini-based dressing would also work very well. Earthy mushrooms love creamy, sticky tahini and its toasty flavour.

+ Romaine or gem lettuce could replace the butterhead, and if you are not in the mood for salad you could pair it with chicken or pork.

Crispy Fried Aubergine, Chilli Sauce & Garlic Yoghurt

Aubergines (eggplants) are funny creatures. The window in which they are perfect – as opposed to undercooked (one of the worst things texturally) or completely overcooked (and more mush than vegetable) – is incredibly small. In the case of this dish, you will be safe in the knowledge that any overcooking will be made up for with the texture of the crisp, buttery breadcrumbs.

Chilli and garlic yoghurt are a match made in heaven, but if you prefer taking your condiment flavours to another part of the world, then I would fully encourage you to do so. Aubergines are originally from South and East Asia, so it would seem a logical step to seek your flavours there.

Serves 4 V

2 large or 4 small aubergines (eggplants)
plain (all-purpose) flour, for dusting
2 eggs, whisked
250g (9oz) panko breadcrumbs
clarified butter or ghee, for frying
2 Tbsp lilliput capers, rinsed and dried
sea salt flakes (kosher salt)

For the chilli sauce
3 banana shallots, roughly chopped
6 garlic cloves, roughly chopped
100ml (3½fl oz) extra-virgin olive oil
375g (13oz) Turkish hot pepper paste (aci biber salçasi)
200g (7oz) ripe tomatoes, roughly chopped
100g (3½oz) tomato ketchup
3 Tbsp pickle juice (from any pickles you may have in the fridge)

For the garlic yoghurt
130g (4½oz) thick yoghurt
½ garlic clove, finely grated
1 Tbsp extra-virgin olive oil

Heat the oven to 200°C/180°C fan/400°F/gas mark 6.

Prick the aubergines (eggplants) all over with the tip of a knife. Place the aubergines on a baking sheet lined with foil and place into the oven for 45–60 minutes or until the aubergines are soft to touch. Leave them to cool completely and then carefully peel off the skin, ensuring you keep it whole and the stalk attached. Split the aubergines in half (keeping the stalk attached) and sit in a sieve to let excess liquid drain out.

To make the chilli sauce, blend the shallots and garlic in a food processor to a fine paste. Heat a large wide-based pan over a medium heat and add the shallot paste along with the olive oil. Cook for 10 minutes, stirring occasionally, and ensuring you scrape the bottom of the pan if any sticky bits form (this is the good stuff). Add the pepper paste into the pan and cook for another 5 minutes, stirring a few times.

Put the tomatoes in a food processor and blitz as fine as they will go. Add the blitzed tomatoes, 250ml (9fl oz) water and the ketchup to the pan and turn the heat down to low. Cook for 25–35 minutes or until a thick sauce has formed. Take off the heat and taste to check the seasoning – as the pepper paste contains salt it may not need any.

(continued overleaf...)

Blitz the finished sauce in a food processor again to achieve a smooth finish, if you like. Once cooled, add the pickle juice. This sauce will store in an airtight container in the fridge for 3–4 weeks.

Whisk together the yoghurt, garlic, olive oil and a little salt. Put the flour, egg and breadcrumbs into dishes large enough to hold the aubergine. Season the aubergine a little on both sides using fine salt. Coat the aubergines in the flour, shaking off any excess, then into the egg and then into the panko breadcrumbs, ensuring you push the breadcrumbs onto the aubergine so they stick well. The trick to this crumbing process is to keep one hand dry and one hand wet so you don't end up with clumps.

Heat the oven to 170°C/150°C fan/325°F/gas mark 3.

Fill a large frying pan (skillet) halfway up with clarified butter or ghee and place over a medium–high heat. Once the fat is hot, carefully add the crumbed aubergine, ensuring you lay it away from you to avoid any splatter-related incidents. Fry on one side for 1–2 minutes or until the crumbs are golden brown. Turn over and fry for another 1–2 minutes on the other side. If frying in batches, place each fried aubergine onto a rack with a baking sheet underneath, then place into the oven and warm through for 5 minutes.

Add the capers to the hot pan and fry until crispy. Drain on paper towel.

Sprinkle the aubergines with a little sea salt flakes (kosher salt), pipe or spoon the chilli sauce and garlic yoghurt on top, or serve them on the side as a dip. Sprinkle over the crispy capers.

Ideas & Inspirations

+ The crispy fried aubergines work really well with a tahini-based sauce.

+ If you can't find Turkish hot pepper paste (aci biber salçasi), you can replace it with tomato purée and chilli powder (pul biber, preferably).

+ Fry the aubergines and serve with the dried shrimp and citrus peel sambal (p.66). Top with chopped coriander (cilantro) and spring onions (scallions) and lime wedges.

+ Fried aubergines also go incredibly well with chermoula (p.223) and mayonnaise (p.75).

Recipes: Nightshades & Mushrooms

Cauliflower Polenta, Imam Bayildi & Broccoli

I worked for the magnificent chef Peter Gordon for quite a number of years, after which I left my role as head chef to embark on my journey towards my own restaurant. A series of pop-ups eventually led to a residency in the train arches in Haggerston, East London. At the time there was really nothing going on in the arches, except for the yoga studio next door to my residency from which slightly sweaty clients would come to have lunch each day. This dish is from that time. I'm not a fan of polenta by any stretch of the imagination, so I really am not sure what possessed me to come up with this. As it turns out, I very much enjoy this dish and I look back fondly on creating it during that time: it's pure comfort, like a chilli-spiked, warming, and slightly addictive hug.

Imam bayildi translates as the 'imam fainted' (because the dish was so good). Although this particular recipe is not made in the traditional way – the aubergine is more commonly stuffed, and doesn't have as rich a texture as mine has, owing to its pepper paste content – I genuinely like to think that the imam would have fainted after mine nonetheless. If you don't like it hot, use less chilli and replace the hot pepper paste with the mild version (or tomato purée).

Serves 4 V

200g (7oz) long-stemmed broccoli
150g (5½oz) feta, crumbled
1 handful of flat-leaf parsley,
 finely shredded

For the imam bayildi
200ml (7fl oz) extra-virgin olive
 oil, plus extra for the polenta
 and broccoli
2 aubergines (eggplants), peeled
 and roughly chopped
3 onions, finely sliced
1 Tbsp fennel seeds, toasted
 and ground
1 Tbsp cumin seeds, toasted
 and ground
1 tsp dried chilli (red pepper) flakes
 or powder (pul biber, preferably)
500g (1lb 2oz) ripe tomatoes,
 roughly chopped

For the imam bayildi, heat a large, lidded pan over a medium heat and add the olive oil, aubergines (eggplants) and onions, with a little salt. Gently cook with a lid on, stirring occasionally, for 20–25 minutes. Add the spices and cook for another 2 minutes, then add the tomatoes and pepper paste and cook, stirring every 10 minutes, for 45–60 minutes with a lid on, or until the tomatoes have collapsed and formed a thick sauce covering the soft aubergines. Add the vinegar and sugar and cook for a further minute. Taste to check the seasoning, and if you feel the mix could do with more sugar or vinegar, adjust accordingly.

For the polenta, place the cauliflower, milk, a little fine salt and the bay leaf in a large pan and place over a medium heat to bring to a simmer. Cook the cauliflower for 20 minutes or until tender. Discard the bay leaf. Spoon out the cauliflower, along with half the milk, into a food processor and blitz to a fine purée. Pour back into the pan of milk.

In a separate pan, with the lid on, cook the onion in a little olive oil and a pinch of salt for 15 minutes or until soft (using a lid will help the onion to cook without colouring). Add the garlic and cook for a further 2 minutes without a lid. Add this to the cauliflower milk. Bring the cauliflower milk up to a gentle

100g (3½oz) Turkish hot pepper
   paste (aci biber salçasi)
1 Tbsp vinegar (sherry, preferably)
1 Tbsp sugar (dark brown, preferably)

For the cauliflower polenta
1 small head cauliflower, cut
   into chunks, stalk discarded
1.25L (44fl oz) whole milk
1 bay leaf
1 onion, finely diced
2 garlic cloves, finely grated
170g (6oz) polenta (cornmeal)
85g (3oz) unsalted butter
70g (2½oz) mascarpone
50g (1¾oz) parmesan (or
   vegetarian alternative), grated

simmer and rain in the polenta (cornmeal), while whisking. Add more seasoning and turn the heat down to low. Cook the polenta, whisking every few minutes, for 20 minutes or until the polenta is cooked through. Take off the heat, stir in the butter, mascarpone and parmesan. Check for seasoning and keep hot with the lid on.

Bring a pan of salted water to the boil and drop in the broccoli. Cook for 2–3 minutes, drain and drizzle with a little olive oil.

To serve, pool some polenta into the centre of a plate and make a well in the middle. Spoon a helping of imam bayildi into the well and top with the broccoli, feta and parsley.

BRAS-SICAS

Napa Cabbage, Cauliflower & Pickled Onions

This was first created out of necessity, just using whatever I had in the house. I was in the mood for something fresh, crunchy and zingy and, in the end, I sort of tossed these things together and was surprised at how good it was. You could use different types of brassicas here and replace the ones I used. The main idea I want you to take from this recipe is that there is nearly always something lurking in the fridge to make a delicious salad – just keep in mind the key building blocks of acid, texture and contrast.

Serves 4 VG

½ napa (Chinese) cabbage,
  finely sliced
½ cauliflower, florets picked and
  finely sliced (with stalk)
50g (1¾oz) good-quality pickled
  onions (I like the ones in balsamic
  vinegar), sliced
1 big handful of coriander (cilantro),
  leaves and stalks shredded
1 red onion, finely sliced
1–2 mild peppers (I like to use long
  green Turkish ones, but any will
  do), cut in half, seeds removed,
  and finely sliced
sea salt flakes (kosher salt)
extra-virgin olive oil
vinegar (red, white, apple cider
  or moscatel)

In a large mixing bowl, add the cabbage, cauliflower, pickled onions, coriander (cilantro), red onion and peppers. Season with sea salt flakes (kosher salt) and drizzle with extra-virgin olive oil and vinegar. Taste the salad. This is where you take over: ask yourself whether it needs more acid, salt or oil. Or, is it perfect as is? Plate up and grind over plenty of black pepper.

Brassicas & Fermented Black Bean Dressing

Brassicas are a lovely way to play around with texture – they work well raw or cooked and the different cooking methods are a lovely contrast to each other. Let your imagination run wild with the varieties of brassicas you could use – think pak choi (bok choy), turnips and their tops, collards, and Brussels sprouts (yes, sprouts are not just for Christmas, and are rather delicious left raw). You can make this even simpler by replacing the brassicas with roasted root vegetables, or even just a selection of raw, finely sliced vegetables.

Serves 4 VG

340ml (11¾fl oz) fermented black bean dressing (p.83)
100g (3½oz) long-stemmed broccoli, ends trimmed
½ cabbage (any or multiple varieties)
¼ cauliflower, florets picked and finely sliced (with stalk)
100g (3½oz) kale, hard stalks removed
extra-virgin olive oil
1 lime, cut into wedges

Prepare the fermented black bean dressing as on page 83.

Place a pan of salted water on to boil. Once boiling, add the broccoli and cook for 1–2 minutes, until just tender but with bite. Scoop out with a slotted spoon and leave to cool.

Take 3–4 of the outer leaves of the cabbage, remove any hard stalks and cut into funky shapes. Cook these in the boiling water, exactly the same as the broccoli, and then leave to cool. Finely shred the inner part of the cabbage raw.

Tear the kale into approximately 2½cm (1in) pieces.

Spread a generous amount of black bean dressing in the centre of a plate. Pile all the vegetables on top, and a drizzle of extra-virgin olive oil. Serve with lime wedges and encourage your guests to squeeze this over before eating.

Ideas & Inspirations

+ This recipe pairs perfectly with roast meats or steamed fish. Personally, I would serve it with pork belly. Ask your butcher for pork belly slices (800g/1lb 12oz for 4 people) with the skin off, sliced 2cm (¾in) wide. Season the slices with fine salt, lay them on a baking sheet lined with baking paper, and place into a preheated oven at 180°C/160°C fan/350°F/gas mark 4 for 45–60 minutes. By this point, the pork should be cooked through and tender but won't have too much colour on it. Turn the oven up to 200°C/180°C fan/400°F/gas mark 6 and coat the pork belly slices in the gochujang glaze from the crispy, sticky chicken and vinegar slaw recipe (p.220). Place back into the oven for 15–20 minutes or until the glaze has caramelized.

+ Or, keep it simple and serve the veggies on a bowl of rice, with a couple of fried eggs on top.

Cabbage, Citrus, Red Onion & Coriander

This is a firm favourite in the various Kiazim households – my own, my sisters' and my mum's. I'm not sure where its origins lie, but if I had to guess I would say it is probably Cypriot in inspiration, as these are ingredients commonly found and used in Cyprus. It's a dish I adore so much that it has graced the menu of my restaurant many times, usually in a big pile sitting next to some barbecued lamb chops smothered in spice paste (p.47) and then slowly grilled. The salad complements and contrasts with smoky, fatty meat beautifully. Ideally, use a mandoline for this to get lovely thin slices of cabbage (just be careful of fingers!) but that is the chef in me. My mum certainly wouldn't use a mandoline, and she uses a selection of incredibly blunt knives, which are perfectly serviceable, according to her. It just goes to show that fancy gadgets don't make or break a good cook. Having said that, a bit of knife sharpening now and then never hurt anyone, Mum.

Serves 4 VG

¼ red cabbage, finely sliced
¼ white cabbage, finely sliced
2–3 oranges, mandarins or both,
    peeled and cut into chunks,
    excess juice reserved
1 red onion, finely sliced
1 big handful of coriander (cilantro),
    shredded
extra-virgin olive oil
1 lemon, juiced
sea salt flakes (kosher salt)

In a large bowl, add the cabbage, oranges (including any excess juice from the peel or chopping board), red onion and coriander (cilantro). Drizzle over some olive oil, squeeze in the lemon juice and season with sea salt flakes (kosher salt). Using your hands, mix the salad thoroughly (this is important!), and taste to see if it is balanced to your liking. Adjust as necessary.

Charred Hispi, Yoghurt, Apple Salsa & Bergamot

This dish just has it all: it is unusual and completely indulgent and will blow any guests' socks off. The yoghurt sauce is probably one of my favourite go-to sauce recipes. Even that sauce by itself is worth making, I promise, and it will go well with anything you would normally use a cream sauce for.

Bergamot is such a special citrus and has the most insane and irresistible perfume. Here, and in most of my recipes, I only use the skin for zesting and the peel for infusing into something; the incredibly sour juice could be used in a marinade that calls for a citrus fruit or as a squeeze over a piece of fish where you would normally use lemon, but on its own, it really is almost unpalatable.

If you were going to be lighting a barbecue anyway (as I recommend you should whenever the weather allows it – spring, summer or autumn) then it would be rude not to give your cabbage a lick of smoke. You could serve this as a starter as part of your barbecue.

Serves 4 V

1 hispi cabbage
extra-virgin olive oil
50g (1¾oz) unsalted butter
1 Tbsp dried chilli (red pepper) flakes (pul biber, preferably)
1 apple, diced
50g (1¾oz) almonds, toasted and chopped
1 small handful of flat-leaf parsley, finely shredded
sea salt flakes (kosher salt)
vinegar (red, white, apple cider or moscatel)
1 bergamot

For the yoghurt sauce
2 Tbsp extra-virgin olive oil
2 banana shallots, finely diced
2 garlic cloves, roughly chopped
1 tsp thyme leaves
100ml (3½fl oz) white wine
150ml (5fl oz) double (heavy) cream
5 Tbsp thick yoghurt

To make the sauce, in a small pan, add the extra-virgin olive oil and warm over a medium-low heat. Add the shallots and cook, stirring every few minutes, for 15 minutes or until the shallots are a deep golden brown. Add the garlic, thyme and a little salt and continue to cook for 2 minutes. Pour in the wine and cook until the liquid has reduced by two thirds. Add the double (heavy) cream and reduce by another third, stirring the pan every few minutes. Take the pan off the heat and leave for 5 minutes. Pour the mix into a blender, add the yoghurt and immediately blitz to form a smooth sauce, adjusting the seasoning if necessary. Keep warm but don't let the sauce boil, or it will split.

Heat the oven to 220°C/200°C fan/425°F/gas mark 7.

Remove any dark green outer leaves from the cabbage and cut it into 4 wedges. Cut away most of the stalk but leave a little so the wedge stays intact. You can either roast these on a baking sheet or cook them in a pan in the oven – the latter is my preferred method to ensure charred edges. In a large, ovenproof frying pan (skillet) add a little olive oil and place over a high heat.

(continued on page 177…)

Add the cabbage wedges to the pan and season with fine salt. Cook until browned on one side, flip over to the other edge and then place the whole pan in the oven. Cook for 10–15 minutes or until the cabbage is soft. You can test this by inserting a skewer or the tip of a small knife in the thickest part to see if it comes out easily.

Melt the butter in a small pan and continue to cook over a gentle heat until it turns golden brown. Take off the heat, strain through a fine sieve and then add the dried chilli (red pepper) flakes.

In a small bowl, combine the apple with the almonds, parsley and a pinch of sea salt flakes (kosher salt). Dress with olive oil and vinegar to your liking – I like to make the salsa quite sharp to cut through the richness of the sauce.

Spoon the yoghurt sauce onto a plate, top with a cabbage wedge, scatter over the salsa, pour over a little chilli butter and then, finally, finely grate over the zest of the bergamot.

───────

Ideas & Inspirations

+ Bergamot adds such a unique perfume but if you can't get hold of one (try good local markets or your friendly restaurant supplier), you can replace it with lime.

+ You can use any cabbage and any nuts you would like. I love using January King cabbage when it's in season – you may just need to roast the wedges for 3–4 minutes longer, as they are slightly chunkier.

+ Instead of cabbage, you could roast quarters of cauliflower or broccoli in exactly the same way.

+ You could serve the roasted cabbage wedges with nut butter and nut vinaigrette (p.122).

+ If you are taking my advice and at least make the yoghurt sauce (and I know you will), serve it with some lamb cutlets. Get 2–3 cutlets per person and season well with fine salt. Heat a large frying pan (skillet) over a medium–high heat, add in a little drizzle of neutral oil and place the cutlets into the pan, fat-side down, for 1–2 minutes or until golden. Cook the cutlets on either side for 1–2 minutes – they'll be pink, so cook them longer if you want them more well-done. Serve with a pool of the yoghurt sauce and scatter over buttered crumbs and sour shallots (p.43), with 1 tsp dried mint mixed into them.

Warm Savoy Cabbage, Peas & Bacon

I was having lunch in a café in Sweden and a warm salad similar to this landed in front of me. I really wasn't expecting it to be anything special. I should have known better: that whole trip to Sweden had been one surprise after another, from racing across ice-covered lakes on snowmobiles, cooking bacon pancakes over an open fire on top of a snowy mountain-peak, and grating dried reindeer over almost any dish in need of something special, in a hut where the snow came up to the eaves. I was being shown around the country by two Swedish

powerhouses, Lena and Fia, where even casual lunches were anything but casual.

That first forkful sang of the warm, sweet pea purée with the texture of savoy cabbage and a lovely hit of acidity from the shallots. I remember jotting down the combination to use at a later date, and here it is. This is a tribute. I'm not sure that original dish had bacon in it, but I decided a little bacon fat infused into a dressing is no bad thing at all.

Serves 4

1 small or ½ large savoy cabbage
500g (1lb 2oz) peas, fresh and
    podded or frozen and defrosted
extra-virgin olive oil
1–2 banana shallots, finely diced
150g (5½oz) smoked pancetta
    lardons or 8 rashers smoked
    streaky bacon, sliced
2 carrots, peeled and diced
2 garlic cloves, finely grated
1 Tbsp thyme leaves
sea salt flakes (kosher salt)
20g (1oz) flat-leaf parsley,
    finely shredded
vinegar (red, white, apple cider
    or moscatel)

Place a pan of salted water on to boil. Remove the core of the cabbage and cut into random-sized shapes. Place into the boiling water for 2 minutes or until the cabbage is tender. Use a slotted spoon to scoop out and allow to cool slightly.

In the same pan of boiling water, place 300g (10½oz) of the peas and boil for 1 minute. Scoop out the peas and place straight into a high-speed blender with a little salt and a splash of the boiling water. Blitz as fine as you wish and keep warm while you prepare the final part. For a silky smooth purée, pass through a fine sieve.

In a pan with a tight-fitting lid, add a little splash of olive oil along with the shallots, pancetta and carrots. Cook over a medium heat for 5–10 minutes or until the vegetables have softened, using the lid to create a little steam. Remove the lid and turn the heat up slightly. Add the garlic and thyme and continue to cook for 1–2 minutes. Add the remaining 200g (7oz) peas, cover with the lid and cook for a further 2 minutes. Remove from the heat and season with sea salt flakes (kosher salt). Add the parsley and enough olive oil and vinegar to thoroughly dress the peas.

To serve, toss together the pea mix with the cabbage and taste to ensure you are happy with the seasoning and dressing. Pile this up over the pea purée.

Verjus Cabbage, Kapuska & Sea Vegetables

Kapuska is a hearty, cabbage-based Turkish stew. 'Kapuska' is the Russian word for cabbage, and similar dishes exist in Russia and other countries that border the Black Sea. This large body of water is somewhat of a transmission vessel for ingredients and dishes, migrants and traders, partnerships and strife. I think it is very likely that the idea of kapuska travelled from one region to another; in turn, it now travels from me to you.

Serves 4

1L (35fl oz) verjus glaze (p.40)

4–5 Tbsp cured beef fat, diced (p.60, optional)

1 small white cabbage

sea salt flakes (kosher salt)

4 Tbsp soft cheese

1 Tbsp wholegrain mustard

2 big handfuls of sea vegetables such as samphire, sea aster, monk's beard and sea beets

2 celery sticks, finely sliced

(continued on page 177…)

Heat the oven to 170°C/150°C fan/325°F/gas mark 3 and prepare the verjus glaze (page 40) and cured beef fat (page 60). Cut the cabbage into 4 wedges. Remove 6–8 layers of the outer leaves of each wedge, shred these leaves finely and set aside. Cut any discoloured bits away from each wedge and remove some of the stalk, ensuring you keep a little, so the wedge stays intact.

For the kapuska, heat a large, ovenproof pan over a high heat, add a splash of neutral oil and season the beef with fine salt. Pop in the pan and caramelize on all sides so the pieces turn a deep brown colour. Scoop out the beef to a plate, pour away the used oil and add half the extra-virgin olive oil. Add the carrot, celery and onion and cook over a high heat. Once the vegetables are browned, add the rest of the olive oil, season with salt and cook for 10–15 minutes or until they are soft. Covering the pan with a lid will help to create a little steam and speed up the process.

Increase the heat, add the sherry vinegar and half the wine to deglaze the pan − scratch off any bits stuck to the bottom of the pan using a wooden spoon (they are the good bits). Cook until all the liquid evaporates.

Add the garlic, herbs, spices and both the tomato and pepper pastes. Stir and cook for 2–3 minutes, before adding the remaining wine. Bring to the boil, add the beef back to the pan with 5–6 Tbsp water. Cover the pan with foil or a lid and place in the oven to cook for 2 hours or until the meat is very tender and falling apart.

(continued on page 177…)

Ideas & Inspirations

+ You can usually find verjus, to make the verjus glaze, online or at a wine store. If not, use vegetable glaze (p.39).

+ A bowl of just the kapuska with some pasta, or beans or rice will make you very happy.

+ If you're not tempted to cure your own beef fat, there are excellent cured meats online or in stores, from beef bacon to guanciale. Give them the same treatment: crisp it up and sprinkle over.

For the kapuska

neutral oil

300g (10½oz) beef (neck, shin
    or chuck), chopped into 2.5cm
    (1in) cubes

3 Tbsp extra-virgin olive oil,
    plus extra for the sea vegetables

1 carrot, finely diced

1 celery stick, finely diced

1 onion, finely diced

1 Tbsp sherry vinegar (if you can't
    find, use any vinegar)

125ml (4fl oz) white wine

2 garlic cloves, finely chopped

1 tsp rosemary, finely chopped

1 tsp thyme leaves, finely chopped

1 bay leaf, torn

1 tsp dried chilli (red pepper)
    flakes (pul biber, preferably)

1 tsp fennel seeds, toasted
    and ground

1 tsp coriander seeds, toasted
    and ground

1 heaped Tbsp tomato purée

1 heaped Tbsp Turkish mild pepper
    paste (tatli biber salçasi); if you
    can't find it, replace with
    tomato purée

sugar, to taste

Remove the kapuska from the oven. Shred the beef using two forks, add back to the pan and stir. Check for seasoning – add in a pinch of sugar and an extra splash of sherry vinegar, if you like. Place the pan over a medium heat and add the shredded cabbage and stir. Cover the pan with a lid and cook for 6–10 minutes or until the cabbage is wilted. Take off the heat. Shred the beef using 2 forks, add back to the pan and stir.

Scatter the cured beef fat, if using, over a large baking sheet and place in the oven for 15–20 minutes, stirring every 5 minutes or until the beef is golden brown. Drain through a sieve and then onto paper towel.

Bring the verjus glaze up to the boil, in an ovenproof wide-based pan, then turn down to a simmer. Add the cabbage wedges along with a little fine salt and cook for 2 minutes on each side. Take off the heat, cover the pan with foil and place in the oven for 20–30 minutes or until the cabbage is cooked through. You can test if the cabbage is cooked by inserting a skewer or the tip of a small knife in the thickest part to see if it comes out easily. Remove the cabbage and drain on paper towel. If you like, you can sear the drained cabbage wedges in a large dry frying pan (skillet) over a high heat, so the edges are a little charred, but this is an optional step. Reduce the glaze down to a syrup, then coat the cabbage wedges in the glaze and season with sea salt flakes (kosher salt).

Combine the soft cheese and mustard together in a bowl and season with sea salt flakes.

Pick through the samphire and monk's beard and pick off any woody stems. Slice any large sea beets or sea aster into smaller pieces. In a small bowl combine the sea vegetables and celery and dress with olive oil.

Pile the kapuska into the centre of your plate. Add the cabbage wedges just off centre, place a quenelle or dollop of mustard cream to the side, and top the cream with the sea vegetables. Scatter over the cured beef fat, if using.

Kale, Caramelized Celeriac & Cacioricotta

Tho purée for this recipe is rich and decadent and worthy of any special-occasion dinner. But even without it, a selection of beautiful brassicas dressed and with a generous grating of cheese all over will make a special mid-week meal.

Serves 4 V

6–8 Tbsp caramelized celeriac (celery root) purée (p.52)

extra-virgin olive oil

½ hispi cabbage, halved lengthwise

4 big handfuls of kale, stalks removed and leaves torn into pieces

40g (1½oz) Brussels sprouts, cut in half and finely sliced

sea salt flakes (kosher salt)

vinegar (red, white, apple cider or moscatel)

1 kohlrabi, peeled and sliced into matchsticks

50g (1¾oz) cacioricotta cheese

½ pomegranate, seeds picked

50g (1¾oz) pistachios, toasted and chopped

Heat the oven to 200°C/180°C fan/400°F/gas mark 6. Prepare the caramelized celeriac (celery root) purée as on page 52.

Place a large, ovenproof frying pan (skillet) over a high heat and drizzle in some olive oil. Add the cabbage, cut-side down, and cook for 3–4 minutes or until the cabbage has a deep caramelized colour. Turn the cabbage over and season with a little fine salt, then place into the oven for 15 minutes. Leave the cabbage to cool and then cut out the core of the cabbage and slice into large strips.

In a large bowl, add the kale and sprouts, season with sea salt flakes (kosher salt) and dress with olive oil and vinegar to your liking. Massage the dressing into the kale and sprouts, using your hands, for a minute. Now add the kohlrabi and roasted cabbage and mix. Taste to ensure the salad has enough salt and dressing. Adjust if necessary.

To plate, spoon the warm caramelized celeriac purée in the bottom of a bowl and top with a big handful of the salad. Grate over a generous helping of the cacioricotta, and sprinkle with the pomegranate seeds and pistachios.

Ideas & Inspirations

+ If you can't find cacioricotta, try a hard goat's cheese, manchego, pecorino or parmesan.

+ Different colours of kale are a lovely way of adding visual contrast to the dish.

+ Try it with a caramelized cauliflower purée (p.52) and some raw shaved cauliflower in the salad.

Kohlrabi, Green Papaya & Salted Coconut

Coconut milk and lime leaves are best friends. The aroma and acidity of the lime leaves infuses so perfectly into rich coconut milk, and it makes the perfect dressing or sauce (try a cold noodle salad piled on top of a pool of the salted coconut sauce).

I fell in love with green papaya and green mangoes as a young chef, at a time when I was completely naïve to the fact they could even be eaten. I loved them for their unique sour crunchiness, and they ended up in many salads I made back in those days. I accept they aren't always the easiest to find, although most Asian supermarkets will stock them (along with the lime leaves). Alternatively, you could pair the kohlrabi with some shredded white cabbage for a similar texture.

Serves 4 VG

1 x 400ml (14fl oz) can
    coconut milk

2 lime leaves (fresh, dried or frozen)

½ Tbsp sea salt flakes (kosher salt)

½–1 lime, juiced

1 kohlrabi, peeled

400g (14oz) green papaya,
    peeled and seeds removed

1 small handful of mint,
    leaves picked

1 small handful of coriander
    (cilantro), leaves picked

Place the coconut milk and lime leaves in a small saucepan and place over a medium heat. Bring to a simmer and reduce the liquid by a third. Strain through a sieve and add the salt and lime juice. Allow to cool to room temperature.

Slice the kohlrabi and papaya into thin strips using a knife or mandoline. Combine with the herbs in a bowl and toss with the coconut dressing to serve.

ALLIUMS

Charred Onions, Pomegranate Dressing, Sumac & Parsley

This recipe is inspired by those gorgeous onion salads you will find in Turkish kebab restaurants. It is also very much a take on the salads I ate all throughout my younger years at family barbecues, of which there were a lot. The beautiful tang from the pomegranate in the dressing and the sumac work really well to cut through the fat of a lamb chop. Ideally, you would grill these onions over hot coals for a smoky flavour but, fear not, they will do just fine in a frying pan. They go well with any sort of protein, or you could toss them along with the dressing through a salad. Serve them with bread or on toast (maybe even croutons… you know how I love a crouton!) and you can mop up all of those gorgeous juices.

Serves 4 VG

4 small onions, quartered
sea salt flakes (kosher salt)
2–4 Tbsp pomegranate dressing
   (p.82)
25g (1oz) parsley, leaves picked
1 tsp sumac

Place a dry frying pan (skillet) over a high heat. Put the onions into the pan, cut-side down, and leave them for 4–5 minutes, each side, to blacken. Alternatively, place the onions under a preheated grill (broiler), cut-side up, and cook that way. Either way, don't disturb them too much while cooking – you want them to char, while still retaining some bite.

Separate out the onion layers into a serving dish, and season with sea salt flakes (kosher salt) to taste. Drizzle over the dressing generously, scatter with the parsley and dust over the sumac.

All the Onions on Toast

Tropea onions are the sweeter, crunchier and altogether more refined cousins of the spring onion (scallion), traditionally grown in the Calabrian region (the toe of the boot of Italy, that is). They're a fine sort and they shine when treated simply, served raw with a good glug of Italian olive oil and some bread. When I discovered them as a young chef they brought me right back to my grandmother's onion salads: pungent, irresistible, well-dressed affairs, best eaten sitting under a Cypriot lemon tree. The best bit, hands-down, is mopping up the salad bits and juices left at the bottom of the bowl. So good was this bit, in fact, that I was compelled to create a recipe around it.

For this recipe, use any variety of onions – have a little look around the market, in your local, or at the back of your pantry to see what you can find. You can shorten this recipe if you'd like by only using some of the cooking methods – just smash a piece of toast with the onion purée, for example, or go purist with just the onion salad – but absolutely key is the contrasting crunch of the bread to soak up all the juices (and get all soft and delectable around the edges) and the use of a good vinegar (your choice).

Serves 4 V

6–8 Tbsp caramelized onion
    purée (p.52)
2 charred onions (p.183)
1 crispy shallots serving (p.48)
1 onion (red, spring/scallion
    or tropea), finely sliced
1 banana shallot, finely sliced
2 Tbsp vinegar (red, white,
    apple cider or moscatel)
1 big handful of mixed herbs
    (parsley, chives, coriander/
    cilantro, tarragon), leaves picked
2 handfuls of mixed salad leaves
4–5 Tbsp extra-virgin olive oil
sea salt flakes (kosher salt)
4 slices good-quality bread
1 garlic clove, peeled

Prepare the purée (page 52), the charred onions (page 183) and the crispy shallots (page 48).

In a bowl, mix together the sliced onion and banana shallot with the vinegar and leave for 10–15 minutes. This will mellow the pungency and harshness of the raw shallot. Add the herbs and salad leaves, 3 Tbsp olive oil and a pinch of sea salt flakes (kosher salt), and mix.

Toast the slices of bread until golden brown and crisp. While still warm, rub the clove of garlic on either side of the toast, season with sea salt flakes and drizzle with extra-virgin olive oil.

Warm through the onion purée and smear over the slices of toast. Be generous. Top with petals of charred onion and pile the onion salad on top. Sprinkle with crispy shallots and season generously with freshly ground black pepper.

Smoked Haddock, Leeks & Sherry Caramel

You could use any smoked fish you like for this and all of these flavours will still work – smoked mackerel, for example, which would just need a bit of warming through, with a good knob of butter in the oven. Fishmongers generally tend to be quite chatty and helpful (at least, mine is), so pop in to see your local one and make sure to ask them what they have in the smoked department. There is no shame at all in using good-quality canned beans, if you prefer. If you do, just boil the leeks in water for 15 minutes or until cooked through and then add to the beans. If you're short on time or motivation, instead of making sherry caramel, you could just dress the salad leaves with sherry vinegar and olive oil. It pays to have a really good sherry vinegar in your cupboard, either way.

Serves 4

3–4 Tbsp citrus dressing (p.79)

2 Tbsp sherry caramel (p.64)

2 leeks

450g (1lb) dried white beans (haricot/navy, butter/lima or coco), soaked overnight

3–4 Tbsp extra-virgin olive oil, plus extra to serve

1 tsp chopped thyme leaves

4 x 140–150g (5–5½oz) portions natural smoked haddock

40g (1½oz) unsalted butter, softened

sea salt flakes (kosher salt)

4 handfuls of mixed salad leaves such as rocket (arugula), lamb's lettuce, watercress

Prepare the citrus dressing (page 79) and the sherry caramel (page 64).

Trim the dark green part of the leeks, and pop to one side. Cut the remaining light green and white part into 2cm (¾in) rounds. Wash both thoroughly – sand is often hiding in the folds.

Drain the beans and tip into a large pan with the dark green leek trimmings. Cover, up to approximately 8cm (3in) over the beans, with water. Place over a high heat and bring up to the boil. Once boiling, turn the heat down to a gentle simmer and skim off any scum, with a spoon, that may have floated to the top. Simmer the beans for 30 minutes. Add the remaining sliced leeks and continue to cook gently for 20 minutes. Taste some of the beans to ensure they are cooked through – they should be completely tender. If they still have bite, continue to cook until softened. Once cooked, drain and place back into the pan. Remove the dark green parts of the leeks and discard.

While the beans are still warm, season generously with fine salt and freshly ground black pepper, drizzle with the 3–4 Tbsp of extra-virgin olive oil and add the thyme. Stir thoroughly and allow to cool to room temperature.

(continued overleaf...)

Meanwhile, heat the oven to 200°C/180°C fan/400°F/ gas mark 6 and line a large baking sheet with baking paper. Smear the smoked haddock portions with the butter (get handsy with them) and season with sea salt flakes (kosher salt). Place the haddock onto the baking sheet, skin side-up, and into the oven for 8–12 minutes. Check the fish is cooked by inserting a skewer or the tip of a knife into the thickest part of a portion for 3 seconds, and then placing the skewer or knife onto your skin just above your thumb joint. If it feels just warm on your skin, then the fish is cooked; if it feels cold, cook for a little longer. Taking the fish out of the oven when it is just warm will mean it finishes cooking while it rests.

In a bowl, coat the salad leaves with 3–4 Tbsp of citrus dressing and a pinch of sea salt flakes. Don't faff about with spoons or forks, I recommend using your hands to get a nice even coating.

Place some cooled beans and leeks in the centre of a plate, drizzle with a little olive oil and season with salt and black pepper. Top with some of the salad, slightly off centre.

Peel the skin away from the haddock and use a fish slice to pick the fish up and place onto the beans. Drizzle over the sherry caramel to finish.

Ideas & Inspirations

+ The baked smoked haddock in this recipe goes brilliantly with potato salad. Try it with spiced mayo (p.75), egg borani (p.206) and chermoula (p.233) in particular.

+ Flake the baked haddock through the warm savoy cabbage, peas & bacon (p.173).

+ Swap out the beans and leeks for butter beans, paprika & piquillo peppers (p.199).

Sweetbreads, Braised Garlic & Samphire

I know offal (variety meat) is not everyone's favourite. I think they could do with a rebrand; the name certainly doesn't help it along. Having said that, sweetbreads are a pretty good entry-level type of offal, as they have a mellow, chicken-like flavour. A classic way of treating them is to simmer the sweetbreads in water, removing the membrane, coating them in flour,

egg and breadcrumbs and frying them. They are the best chicken nuggets (that are not chicken) you'll ever have.

This recipe is one of my favourites, and the acidity of the shallots and samphire, and the crispy croutons, contrast beautifully with those lovely buttery sweetbreads.

Serves 4

2 Tbsp Kyseri spice mix (p.56)
150g (5½oz) braised garlic (p.63)
80g (2¾oz) small croutons (p.46)
1 small banana shallot, finely
   sliced into rounds
1 Tbsp vinegar (red, white,
   apple cider or moscatel)
350–400g (12–14oz) sweetbreads
   (lamb or veal)
1 Tbsp neutral oil
50g (1¾oz) unsalted butter
4 heaped Tbsp thick yoghurt,
   room temperature
90g (3¼oz) samphire, trimmed
   of any hard stems
1 Tbsp finely sliced mint
extra-virgin olive oil

Prepare the Kyseri spice mix (page 56), the braised garlic (page 63) and the croutons (page 46).

Put the sliced shallot in a small bowl or jar, cover in the vinegar, season with salt and leave for at least 30 minutes.

Remove the sinew from the sweetbreads, season with fine salt and dust heavily with the Kyseri spice mix on one side. Heat up a large frying pan (skillet) over a high heat and add the neutral oil. Place the sweetbreads in the pan spice-dusted-side down and cook for 1–2 minutes or until the sweetbreads are a deep golden colour. At this point the pan will be very hot, so remove from the heat for 30 seconds or so while you flip over the sweetbreads, so you don't overcook them. Place the pan back on the heat and add in 30g (1oz) of the butter. Once the butter is foaming, keep spooning it back over the sweetbreads and cook for a further 1–2 minutes, until they feel firmer.

Scoop out the sweetbreads, place onto a paper towel, and pour away the excess butter. Once the pan has cooled down for a minute, add the braised garlic, along with 30ml (1fl oz) water, bring up to a simmer, then stir through the remaining 20g (¾oz) butter and simmer to thicken the sauce. Turn the heat off, add the sweetbreads back to the pan and coat in the sauce.

To serve, spoon yoghurt on one side of a plate. Spoon around the sweetbreads and garlic and scatter over the samphire and croutons. Place a few rounds of the sour shallots over the top, sprinkle with the mint, and finish with a drizzle of extra-virgin olive oil.

Ideas & Inspirations

+ Instead of the Kyseri spice mix, you could use curry powder to dust the sweetbreads (or make your own blend of spices).

+ If you really aren't convinced on giving the sweetbreads a go, you have my permission to use chicken thigh instead. Cut the chicken into approximately 3cm (1¼in) square pieces and cook in the same way, but give them an extra minute on each side.

+ Lamb also works really well with all the flavours here. Cut 4–5 slashes into a bone-in shoulder of lamb and rub it all over with the Kyseri spice mix and a generous amount of fine salt. Place into a roasting tray on top of thickly (2cm/¾in) sliced onions, and roast at 170°C/150°C fan/325°F/gas mark 3 for 5–6 hours, or until the meat is beautiful and gnarly, and easily pulls away from the bone. Serve with the braised garlic and yoghurt, and a salad of the samphire, sour shallots, croutons and herbs.

+ The sauce goes great with pasta, too. Just pop some spaghetti on to boil. Meanwhile, warm through the braised garlic in a large frying pan and stir in 30g (1oz) of butter. Drain the pasta and add to the pan along with a few tablespoons of the pasta cooking water (this helps the sauce emulsify). If you're feeling confident, toss the pasta and sauce together (although stirring will do just fine) over a medium heat. Serve with plenty of grated parmesan, freshly ground black pepper and picked thyme leaves over the top.

Ideas & Inspirations

+ Place a 200g (7oz) block of good-quality feta in a ceramic baking dish and drizzle over a little olive oil. Bake in the oven at 200°C/180°C fan/400°F/gas mark 6 for 12–16 minutes, or until a little golden on the top. Spoon the warm leeks and mushrooms over the top.

+ Toss the leeks and mushrooms through some noodles or pasta. Serve with a side salad.

+ Serve the leeks and mushrooms alongside any meat or fish. A piece of white roasted fish, such as hake, would be ideal.

+ For a veggie-friendly option, dice some tofu, toss in cornflour (cornstarch) and fry in a neutral oil until crisp. Serve with the leeks and mushrooms, some chilli dressing (p.81) and a good sprinkling of crispy shallots (p.48).

Slow-Cooked Leeks & Oyster Mushrooms

This recipe will pretty much take what you throw at it, so use any mushrooms you like. Mushroom foragers at markets will often have some really beautiful mushrooms like ceps or chanterelles that are a little bit older and need to be eaten sooner rather than later – scoop them up for a lower price, they will work beautifully in this recipe.

Serves 4 V

2 large or 4 small leeks, green tops
   cut off
extra-virgin olive oil
2 big handfuls of coriander (cilantro)
   with stalks
1 big garlic clove
1 chilli
1 lime, zested and juiced
300g (10½oz) oyster mushrooms,
   torn into pieces
1 Tbsp butter
sea salt flakes (kosher salt)

Dice the leeks into approximately 2cm (¾in) dice and wash thoroughly.

Heat a large, lidded wide-based pan over a medium heat and add 5–6 Tbsp olive oil – it should be enough to cover the bottom of the pan. Add in the leeks, season with fine salt and, once you hear them starting to fry, turn the heat down a little and place a lid on top. Sweat the leeks gently, stirring occasionally, for 25 minutes or until soft.

Roughly chop the coriander (cilantro) leaves and stalks, garlic and chilli, place into a small blender with the lime zest, and add a glug of olive oil. Glug is one of those words that could mean anything to anyone, but I reckon it should be about the quantity to escape from the bottle when it takes in its first 'glug' of air. More is better than less, in any case. Blitz to form a paste, and add a little more olive oil if need be. Set aside.

Place a large frying pan (skillet) over a high heat for 1 minute. Add another glug of oil followed by the mushrooms. Fry for 2–3 minutes, so they get a little colour and cook through, at which point they're almost ready. Add in the butter and season with sea salt flakes (kosher salt). Scoop out and drain on paper towel.

To serve, stir the coriander paste into the warm leeks along with the lime juice. Spoon onto a plate and top with the mushrooms.

BEANS, GRAINS & PULSES

Spicy Green Beans, Brown Rice & Pork

This recipe has some ingredients you might not necessarily have knocking about your store cupboard, but sourcing them is half the fun. Going to Chinatown and getting lost in a shop of fabulous ingredients is one of my favourite things to do (prepare to bring some things home to experiment with). These green beans are worth the effort: they are so good you could eat them off a shoe.

Serves 4

240g (8½oz) brown rice

neutral oil, for frying

500g (1lb 2oz) pork mince (ground pork)

2 garlic cloves, finely grated

6cm (2½in) ginger, peeled and finely grated

2–3 Tbsp soy sauce

1 Tbsp palm sugar or dark brown sugar

30g (1oz) unsalted butter

1 big handful of coriander (cilantro), leaves picked

2 spring onions (scallions), finely sliced

For the spicy green beans

2 Tbsp neutral oil

5 banana shallots, finely sliced

3 garlic cloves, finely grated

6cm (2½in) ginger, peeled and finely grated

1–2 chillies, finely sliced with seeds

1 tsp Chinese five spice

450g (1lb) green beans, ends trimmed, cut into 4

90g (3¼oz) kecap manis

90g (3¼oz) yellow bean sauce

5 Tbsp black rice (chinkiang) vinegar

1½ Tbsp sesame oil

2 Tbsp palm sugar or dark brown sugar

1 lime, zested and juiced

Cook the brown rice according to packet instructions.

To make the green beans, heat a large pan with the neutral oil over a medium–high heat. Add the shallots and cook for 5–8 minutes or until the shallots have softened slightly. Add the garlic, ginger and chilli and cook for 2 minutes. Add the five spice and mix through for another minute. Add the green beans, kecap manis, yellow bean paste, black vinegar, sesame oil, sugar and 5 Tbsp water. Make sure everything is spread out evenly in the pan and turn the heat to low. Cook for 5–10 minutes or until the beans are tender and the liquid has reduced to a syrupy consistency. Take off the heat, add the lime juice and zest and check for seasoning. Keep warm.

Heat up a large frying pan or wok over a high heat with a little neutral oil. Add the pork mince (ground pork) and cook for 8 minutes or until any liquid has evaporated and the pork is sizzling. Use a whisk to keep stirring the pork so it breaks up into small pieces. If the pan is dry add in a little more neutral oil followed by the garlic and ginger. Cook for a minute, add in the soy sauce and sugar and continue to cook, stirring thoroughly, for 2–3 minutes or until the pork is a little caramelized. Drain off any excess fat before serving.

Stir the butter into the cooked, hot rice.

To serve, divide the rice between bowls, top with the green beans and pork, and a sprinkling of coriander (cilantro) leaves and spring onions (scallions).

Pickles, Hummus, Garlic Sausage & Granola

This is basically a loaded hummus and by all means take it as inspiration to create your own version. What I want to demonstrate is how grand and luxurious hummus really is. These days, you can find some version of hummus in most supermarkets and shops, but I find these dips rather sad versions of the real thing.

A well-made hummus is sexy and deserves respect, especially as it will gladly hang out with flavours from all around the world, making it incredibly versatile.

Be sure to hunt down good bread, flatbreads or crispy crackers of some description, for all the mopping up that will need to be done.

Serves 4

8–10 Tbsp hummus (p.76)
6–8 Tbsp spiced granola (p.46)
6–8 Tbsp pickles (p.87)
2 garlic sausages (I like to use Turkish sujuk, but you could use chorizo or merguez)
3 Tbsp cooked chickpeas (garbanzo beans), rinsed
1 big handful of herbs such as mint, coriander (cilantro) and parsley, leaves picked
1 big handful of salad leaves such as chicory (endive) or gem
sea salt flakes (kosher salt)
extra-virgin olive oil

Prepare the hummus (page 76), the spiced granola (page 46) and the pickles (page 87).

Dice the garlic sausages into 1cm (½in) pieces. Add to a large frying pan (skillet) over a medium–high heat. Cook for 5–8 minutes or until the sausage is browned and the oil has separated. Add in the chickpeas (garbanzo beans) and warm through.

Place the hummus in a bowl, or bowls, and smear around in a circle using the back of a spoon. Arrange the herbs, salad leaves, pickles and granola around the bowl and season with sea salt flakes (kosher salt), then drizzle over a little extra-virgin olive oil. Finish by spooning the sausage and chickpeas, along with their delicious oil, into the bowl.

Butter Beans, Paprika & Piquillo Peppers

I love this recipe and others of its kind because it's simple, quick and bursting with flavour. You may be under the impression that us chefs either subsist on takeaway (when we aren't working) or make elaborate and creative masterpieces at home every night of the week. Nothing could be less true. We are mere mortals, just like you, and we want to have as much flavour as we can in as little time as possible. This recipe is just that, especially as most of the ingredients will be in your store cupboard.

Serves 4 VG

3 red onions, diced
125ml (4fl oz) extra-virgin olive oil
4 garlic cloves, finely sliced
1 Tbsp dried chilli (red pepper)
   flakes (pul biber, preferably)
1½ Tbsp sweet smoked paprika
1 Tbsp tomato purée
2 x 400g (14oz) canned butter
   (lima) beans, drained and rinsed
5 Tbsp sherry vinegar
300g (10½oz) piquillo peppers,
   rinsed and sliced
sea salt flakes (kosher salt)

In a wide-based pan over a medium heat, caramelize the red onions in 75ml (2½fl oz) of the olive oil for 15 minutes or until they turn golden and soft. Add a little fine salt, the garlic and spices and continue to cook for 2–3 minutes. Add the tomato purée and cook for another minute.

Add the butter (lima) beans and sherry vinegar and reduce the liquid by half over a medium heat. Turn the heat off. Add the piquillo peppers and the remaining olive oil and season with sea salt flakes (kosher salt) to serve.

Ideas & Inspirations

+ These beans are great in salads. Let the mix cool and then toss through a selection of salad leaves and herbs. Perk up the leaves with a little olive oil and vinegar, and some crispy lavash (p.47) on top.

+ Have a big bowl of the beans with a simple dollop of thick yoghurt and some crusty bread.

+ Serve the beans on a bed of rice with some crispy fried eggs.

+ Prepare the recipe and pour into a baking dish. Place fillets of white fish (such as hake or pollock) on top. Bake in a preheated oven, at 200°C/180°C fan/400°F/gas mark 6 for 10–15 minutes, depending on the size of the fish.

Freekeh, Crispy Prawns & Pistachio

This is a variation on a dish I once served at my restaurant, Oklava. I asked my front-of-house team to encourage people to eat the prawns (shrimp) shell and all, because people's gut-reaction when they see a prawn shell is to want to peel it off. That's a shame, because there is a lot of texture and flavour to be had.

Serves 4

extra-virgin olive oil, for frying
2 onions, diced
4 garlic cloves, finely chopped
150g (5½oz) freekeh, rinsed
neutral oil, for deep frying
12 raw tiger prawns (shrimp),
    shell on
plain (all-purpose) flour, for dusting
40g (1½oz) unsalted butter
1 big handful of mint, parsley and
    tarragon, chopped
60g (2¼oz) pistachios, toasted
    and ground to a crumb in a
    food processor
1 lemon, cut into wedges

Place a large, lidded wide-based pan over a medium-low heat with a big glug of extra-virgin olive oil. Add the onions, season with fine salt and place a lid on top. Sweat the onions, stirring occasionally, for 8–10 minutes or until they're softened with no colour. Add the garlic and cook for a further minute with the lid off. Add the freekeh, 280ml (10fl oz) water and a little more salt and bring to the boil. Once boiling, place a lid on top and turn down the heat to its lowest setting. Cook for 25 minutes or until the freekeh is cooked through but has a little bite.

Meanwhile, set a deep-fat fryer to 180°C/350°F, or heat a large pan filled no more than halfway up with neutral oil over a medium-high heat.

Using a sharp serrated knife, cut the prawns (shrimp) in half through the head and body (see page 202) and remove the intestinal tract – this is the black line that runs the length of the prawn. Season the prawns with fine salt and dust thoroughly in flour.

Check the oil temperature – it should read 180°C/350°F. If you don't have a thermometer you can use a little cube of bread: just drop it into the oil and if it begins to sizzle immediately, then the oil is ready.

Dust any excess flour off the prawns and drop into the hot oil in two batches, to avoid overcrowding the pan. Fry for 2 minutes or until the prawns have turned pink and crispy. Drain on paper towel and season with fine salt.

Stir the butter and herbs through the warm freekeh before spreading over a plate. Top with the pistachio crumbs and crispy prawns, and lemon wedges to serve.

Ideas & Inspirations

+ If the thought of eating prawn (shrimp) shells is not your thing, then this recipe will work with peeled ones (I just compel you to try leaving the heads on), but I promise you that when dusted in flour and deep fried, the prawns (shells and all) become moreish and unexpectedly delicious.

+ Try frying pieces of white fish, such as pollock, hake or cod, dusted in flour in the same way.

+ You could scrap the seafood altogether and serve the freekeh next to a roast chicken. Roast chicken is one of those recipes it pays to have etched into your brain. It may take roasting a couple of birds before you find the recipe you like and rely on. My go-to roast chicken recipe (based on a large chicken) is as follows: heat the oven to 200°C/180°C fan/400°F/gas mark 6 and find a roasting tin that fits the chicken with just a little gap around the edge (too small a tin and you won't get enough colour on the chicken, too big a tin and you will burn all the glorious juices from the chicken). On the bottom of the tin, layer onions sliced into 2cm (¾in) rounds. Stuff the cavity of the chicken with

4–5 garlic cloves, half a lemon and a handful of thyme sprigs. Smear softened butter all over the bird and season generously with fine salt all over. Place the chicken, breast-side down, on top of the onions and place in the oven for 45 minutes. Flip over and cook for another 45 minutes breast-side up. A small chicken will need 30 minutes a side; a medium chicken will need 35 minutes a side. Once cooked – the juices should run clear, with no bleed, when skewered at its thickest parts – leave the chicken to rest in a warm part of the kitchen for 25 minutes before carving.

+ Freekeh is a young green durum wheat, which has been fire roasted and then polished to remove the grains, so it has a gently smoked, nutty flavour and chewy, bouncy texture. You can buy it online or in Middle Eastern supermarkets, but if you can't find it, bulgur wheat also works well. Cook according to packet instructions, as the bulgur will cook quicker and need less liquid than its freekeh friend.

Ideas & Inspirations

+ Serve next to a selection of steamed veggies.
A pile of purple sprouting broccoli is my go-to,
with some spiced crumbs (p.47) sprinkled over.

+ Sit some bone-in chicken thighs (2 per
person) on the top and bake in the oven for
25 minutes for a complete meal.

+ I would normally make a salad next to this,
but if you want to go quick and easy, shred up
some lettuce, add some coriander (cilantro)
leaves and dress with lemon juice and salt.
The freshness of just that will cut through the
richness of the beans really well.

Borlotti Beans, Cured Meat & Prunes

By all means, go ahead and cook the borlotti beans from dried if you wish, but I use canned for this recipe, as I want to show you how to pack loads of flavour into a quick one-pot wonder. This is a lovely combination of things: acidity from the wine to cut through the sweetness of the prunes, a flavour boost from the gremolata, lots of different textures dancing around your mouth, and the contrast between different flavour profiles (cured meat, fruit, and earthy beans). Highly recommended with toast or crusty bread for extra crunchy texture.

Serves 4

3–4 Tbsp gremolata-ish (p.74)
200–300g (7–10½oz) cured meat such as chorizo, cecina, jamon, pancetta, salami or saucisson
extra-virgin olive oil
2 onions, finely diced
2 carrots, finely diced
2 celery sticks, finely diced
3 garlic cloves, finely chopped
1½ Tbsp thyme or rosemary, leaves finely chopped
150ml (5fl oz) red wine
8 prunes, pitted and cut into 4
1 x 400g (14oz) can chopped tomatoes or passata
1 tsp sugar (dark brown, preferably)
2 x 400g (14oz) cans borlotti beans, drained and rinsed
1 tsp vinegar (red, white, apple cider, balsamic or moscatel)

Prepare the gremolata-ish as on page 74.

Slice your chosen cured meat into slices or small pieces. Heat a large, lidded pan over a medium heat and add 3–4 Tbsp extra-virgin olive oil. Add the onions, carrots, celery and cured meat and season with fine salt and freshly ground black pepper. Pop the lid on the pan and sweat the vegetables, stirring occasionally, for 15–20 minutes or until the vegetables are soft.

Remove the lid and turn up the heat, then add the garlic and half the herbs and cook for 1 minute. Add the red wine and prunes and cook until the wine reduces and there is almost no liquid left. Add the tomatoes and sugar, turn the heat down to low and cook with the lid on for 20 minutes.

Remove the lid again, add the beans and cook for a further 15 minutes with the lid off or until the sauce has thickened and is clinging onto the beans. Adjust the seasoning with salt and freshly ground black pepper and add a little splash of vinegar to finish. Top with the gremolata-ish and the remaining herbs.

Puy Lentils & Egg Borani

Borani is a dip popular in Persian and Turkish cuisine, and in its most basic form it's a combination of thick yoghurt and a vegetable (usually spinach, but it's super adaptable – mushrooms and carrots work well, too). The acidity of the yoghurt is a lovely contrast to the inherent sweetness of the vegetables.

This recipe is a take on the original, but I have chosen to go somewhat off-piste and use eggs. Ideally, use sherry vinegar and be quite bold with it, as you want the extra acidity to cut through the richness of the eggs.

Serves 4 V

250–350g (9–12oz) cooked
   Puy, green or brown lentils
1 red onion, finely diced
1 green (bell) pepper, finely diced
80g (2¾oz) piquillo peppers, diced
1 small handful of flat-leaf parsley,
   finely shredded
vinegar (red, white, apple cider,
   sherry or moscatel)

For the egg borani
4 eggs, room temperature
30g (1oz) unsalted butter
extra-virgin olive oil
1 onion, finely diced
2 garlic cloves, finely grated
a pinch of cumin seeds, toasted
   and ground
a pinch of fennel seeds, toasted
   and ground
a pinch of ground turmeric
3 Tbsp thick yoghurt
sea salt flakes (kosher salt)

For the egg borani, bring a small pan of water up to the boil and gently lower in the eggs to boil for 7 minutes. Drain and cool under cold running water. Peel the eggs and chop into small pieces.

In a small, lidded pan, over a medium heat, melt the butter with a drizzle of olive oil. Add the onion with a pinch of fine salt. Cook the onion with a lid on, stirring occasionally, for 10–15 minutes or until the onion is soft. Take the lid off, add the garlic followed by the ground spices, and cook for 1 minute. Take off the heat and leave the mix to cool for 10 minutes. Stir in the yoghurt and chopped eggs and adjust the seasoning with sea salt flakes and a generous amount of freshly ground black pepper.

In another bowl, combine the lentils, red onion, green (bell) pepper, piquillo peppers and parsley. Season with more sea salt flakes and black pepper and dress with extra-virgin olive oil and vinegar. Taste and adjust accordingly.

Spoon the borani into the centre of a plate and push out with the back of a spoon to form a well. Fill the well with the lentil salad.

Ideas & Inspirations

+ Ditch the lentils and serve the borani on its own, with a pile of croutons or bread for dipping in.

+ For a mega egg sandwich, put the borani between two pieces of toast and add some sliced gherkins in there for extra acidity.

+ I love the borani served with roasted cabbage wedges – use the method in the recipe for charred hispi, yoghurt, apple salsa & bergamot (p.168).

Chickpea, Morcilla & Romaine

La Boqueria market, in the middle of Las Ramblas in Barcelona, is an assault on the senses, in the best way possible. In the morning, the traders, some of whom have worked here for decades, roll up the blinds and reveal a huge array of local produce: fish so fresh their gills are a bright red and their scales a sheen of metal; high piles of leafy vegetables every conceivable colour of green; and the smell of aged ham and freshly-ground coffee abounds. Locals sit and read their papers, there is the comfortable lilt of Spanish and Catalan (and a fair bit of English these days, too), and in between weave the foreign visitors, mouths agape. I was one of them, the first time I went,

and I still am. La Boqueria inspired my love for markets, and now I will visit the market in whichever city I travel to, large or small, but it is a rare occurrence that these markets match the original colour and excitement of La Boqueria.

At the entrance of the market (just on the right, for when you go) is one little 17-stool tapas bar, Pinotxo, run by bow-tie clad Juanito Bayen. I am utterly obsessed with one dish here: chickpeas (garbanzo beans) with morcilla. It is a simple dish but works so well, with a hint of sweetness from raisins, the flavour bomb that is morcilla, the acidity from the vinegars, and the addictive texture of the chickpeas. My recipe is a homage.

Serves 4

extra-virgin olive oil

1 onion, finely diced

2 garlic cloves, finely chopped

¼ tsp ground cinnamon

¼ tsp cumin seeds, toasted and ground

4 morcilla sausages, skins removed

2 x 400g (14oz) cans cooked chickpeas (garbanzo beans), rinsed

2 Tbsp pine nuts, lightly toasted

2 Tbsp sultanas or raisins

1 head romaine lettuce, leaves separated

sea salt flakes (kosher salt)

vinegar (red, white, apple cider or moscatel)

1 handful of flat-leaf parsley, finely shredded

Heat a large frying pan (skillet) over a medium–high heat and add a big glug of extra-virgin olive oil. Add the onion and cook for 6–8 minutes or until slightly softened. Add the garlic and ground spices and cook for another minute.

Remove the onion mix to a bowl, and wipe the pan with paper towel. Place back on the heat and crumble in the morcilla. Cook over a high heat for 5 minutes, breaking up the morcilla with a wooden spoon as it cooks. Add the onion mix back into the pan, along with the chickpeas (garbanzo beans), mix thoroughly and season with fine salt and freshly ground black pepper. Turn the pan down to a medium heat, add the pine nuts and sultanas and continue to cook for 5 minutes. Take off the heat and leave the mix to cool until just warm.

Place the warm morcilla and chickpea mix and the romaine lettuce in a large bowl. Season with sea salt flakes (kosher salt), black pepper, a drizzle of extra-virgin olive oil and a little vinegar. Toss together and plate up. Sprinkle over the parsley, and a little extra salt and olive oil, to serve. It's great with some crusty bread.

POULTRY & MEAT

Pork Laab, Sugar Snaps & Apple

Laab (or larb) is a meat salad of Lao origin. It perfectly combines acid from lime juice, texture from toasted rice, and contrast between the lovely fat of pork mince (ground pork) and the beautiful aromatics and chillies. I am not a laab expert, by any stretch of the imagination, but I am a laab fan and this recipe is an homage.

You don't have to use all the aromatics below, but these are the ones I tend to have in the fridge. Cooking up a batch of laab and keeping it on-hand in the fridge means you'll always have a quick and easy go-to lunch or dinner option. I serve it with rice or lettuce cups for a quick alternative to this sugar snap and apple number.

Serves 4

2 Tbsp rice

neutral oil, for frying

450g (1lb) pork mince (ground pork), alternatively you could use chicken or lamb mince

1 lemongrass, bashed and outer leaves removed (freeze these to use in the recipe on p.245), inner part finely chopped

5cm (2in) ginger, peeled and finely chopped

1–2 chillies, finely sliced, or use dried chilli (red pepper) flakes

2 lime leaves, finely sliced

2 garlic cloves, finely chopped

1 Tbsp palm sugar or dark brown sugar

3 Tbsp fish sauce

1–2 limes

2–3 spring onions (scallions) or Thai red shallots, finely sliced

1 big handful of coriander (cilantro), leaves picked, stalks finely chopped

1 green apple

80g (2¾oz) sugar snap peas

1 big handful of mint leaves

sea salt flakes (kosher salt)

Toast the rice in a dry frying pan (skillet), over a medium heat, for 6–10 minutes or until golden brown. Once the rice has cooled, pound to a coarse powder using a pestle and mortar or in a small blender.

Place a large frying pan or wok over a high heat and add a little neutral oil. Add the pork mince (ground pork) and cook, stirring regularly, to break up the pieces. Cook for 10–15 minutes or until the mince is lightly browned and any water has evaporated.

Add in the lemongrass, ginger, chilli, lime leaves and garlic and continue to cook for 1–2 minutes. If the pan seems a little dry, add a touch more oil to help fry the aromatics. Turn the heat down to medium, add in the sugar and cook for 1–2 minutes. Turn the heat off and leave the mince to cool a little. Add the fish sauce, the juice of 1 lime and a little fine salt. Taste and see if it needs more lime juice, fish sauce, sugar, or chilli. It should be juicy and punchy with the flavours, but balance it to your liking. Stir in the spring onions (scallions) and coriander (cilantro) stalks.

Quarter the apple, cut away the core from each piece and finely slice. Slice the sugar snap peas into fine strips and combine in a bowl with the apple, mint and coriander leaves, and season with sea salt flakes (kosher salt).

Serve the laab in a big pile with the toasted rice scattered over the top. Pile up the salad to the side, serve with some lime wedges and a little extra chilli, if you like it really hot.

Lamb Bacon, Bitter Leaves & Mustard

Served with toast, this makes a great lunch. It works well as a starter, too. The recipe for the dressing is a rough guide, and you should feel free to adjust it to your liking: more mustard, for example, or reduce the vinegar if you would like it less acidic. Regular pork bacon also works.

You could also replace the bitter leaves with dandelion, or leaves like gem lettuce or frisée.

One final note on lamb bacon – keep an eye on it. This stuff is addictive and one moment of casual inattention and you may find your stash has been raided.

Serves 4

16–20 slices lamb bacon (p.60)
neutral oil, for frying
2–3 Tbsp maple syrup
4 big handfuls of bitter leaves,
   such as chicory or radicchio
1 big handful of flat-leaf parsley,
   leaves picked

For the mustard dressing
1 tsp wholegrain mustard or
   Dijon mustard
1 tsp honey
1 small garlic clove, finely grated
2 Tbsp vinegar (red, white,
   apple cider or moscatel)
6 Tbsp extra-virgin oil

Prepare the lamb bacon as on page 60 and slice it as thick as you like.

Heat a large frying pan (skillet) over a high heat. Add a tiny splash of neutral oil and add the bacon slices. Cook until golden and a little crisp on both sides – you may need to do this in batches if your pan isn't big enough. Once all the bacon is cooked, wipe out the pan with paper towel and place back on the heat. Add in the bacon and maple syrup and cook until the bacon is completely coated in the syrup and sticky. Take all the bacon out of the pan immediately to stop it burning.

In a large bowl, make the mustard dressing by whisking together the mustard, honey, garlic and vinegar. While whisking, slowly drizzle in the oil until it is all emulsified. Season with fine salt and freshly ground black pepper and add the bitter leaves and parsley. Coat all the leaves thoroughly and add the bacon slices, to serve.

Seared Bavette, Smoked Anchovy & Gem

I love steak. Every once in a while, I will get a craving. These days, aware of what it is actually needed to rear cattle sustainably and responsibly, and the impact it actually has, I treat this craving with a little ceremony. It is a luxury rather than an everyday meal. I will go and visit my butcher and spend some time picking out a nice cut – they usually have some wine tastings going on in the shop, so I really don't mind spending the time. I shop around for some sides which will equal the steak in flavour. Light the candles, have a glass of red – I'm not saying all meals deserve this sort of ritual, but a little now and then won't hurt.

Serves 4

4 Tbsp miso and lemon dressing (p.84)
3–4 Tbsp crispy shallots (p.48)
4 x 200g (7oz) bavette steaks
neutral oil, for frying
2 heads baby gem, cut in half
100g (3½oz) smoked anchovies
60g (2¼oz) unsalted butter
2 thyme sprigs
1 garlic clove, bashed
sea salt flakes (kosher salt)

Prepare the miso and lemon dressing (page 84) and the crispy shallots (page 48).

Heat a large, heavy frying pan (skillet) over a high heat. If your pan is not big enough to cook all 4 steaks then use 2 pans or cook in pairs and then reheat in the oven. Season the steaks generously with fine salt. Add a good splash of oil into the pan and add the steaks. Cook for 1–2 minutes and then flip over and cook for another 1–2 minutes on the other side. Repeat this process another 2 times so in total the steaks will cook for 4–8 minutes (for rare steaks; cook longer on either side if you liked it more well done). Remove the steaks from the pan(s) and leave to rest on a plate in a warm place in the kitchen for at least 10 minutes.

Place a baby gem half on each plate and dress generously with the miso dressing. Top with the crispy shallots. Split each anchovy in half lengthwise.

Put the frying pan back over a high heat, place the steaks back in and sear on each side for 30 seconds. Add in the butter, thyme sprigs and garlic. Baste the steaks with the foaming butter for another 30 seconds on each side.

Transfer the steaks to plates, top each with 3–4 strips of anchovy and a sprinkling of sea salt flakes (kosher salt). Serve with the dressed gem lettuce.

Ideas & Inspirations

+ Bavette steak does really need to be eaten very pink, otherwise it will be tough. If you are someone who is just not into that level of rare, or who prefers a different cut of steak, then by all means see what is available at your local butcher. I also enjoy cutting the steak into large cubes, seasoning heavily and then searing in a hot pan until they form a crust on all sides. Once rested they end up as little nuggets of joy, and it is an easier way of cooking steak and achieving a pink centre.

+ Use regular anchovies if you can't find smoked, but they are special so do have a look online or in Spanish delis.

+ Other dressings, for example za'atar (p.85), chilli (p.81) and sumac (p.81) also work very well with the lettuce. Or you could freestyle and dress the leaves with a little olive oil, acid of choice and seasoning.

+ One of the potato salads (p.226) would be a winner served with this steak.

+ Instead of the miso dressing, chermoula (p.233) would be great.

Pork, Crackling, Coriander & Palm Sugar Dressing

There is really nothing quite like pork crackling. Even the sound of the skin popping as you take it out of the oven makes my mouth water. This has to be high-quality, sustainably and ethically reared meat, or otherwise I wouldn't bother. What was good for the pig will be good for us.

To be honest, if I'm going to roast a big hunk of pork shoulder with crispy crackling, I don't really want much next to it, other than a good salad of some description. I love carbs as much as the next person, but sometimes they do just get in the way of having more of this pork-ey loveliness. But noodles or a bowl of rice would work well.

Ensure the skin of the pork is very dry. Leave it for at least 24 hours uncovered in the fridge.

Serves 4

100ml (3½fl oz) palm sugar, chilli and lime dressing (p.83)
2kg (4lb 8oz) bone-in pork shoulder, skin scored (ask your butcher to score it for you)
20g (¾oz) coriander (cilantro), shredded
4 spring onions (scallions), finely sliced

Heat the oven to 220°C/200°C fan/425°F/gas mark 7 and prepare the palm sugar, chilli and lime dressing (page 83).

Line a roasting tin (big enough to fit the pork) with 2 layers of foil. Place a piece of baking paper over the foil and sit a rack into the tin.

Season the pork liberally with fine salt and place into the tray. Pour a cup of water on the bottom of the tray and cover the pork with foil. Place in the oven for 1 hour. Remove the foil and turn the oven down to 180°C/160°C fan/350°F/gas mark 4 and cook the pork for a further 2–3 hours or until tender. You can test this by inserting a small knife into the thickest part of the meat and you should feel little resistance. Take the pork out of the oven and leave to rest in a warm part of your kitchen for at least 30 minutes.

Turn the oven up to 240°C/220°C fan/475°F/gas mark 8.

Place the pork back in the oven, for 8–15 minutes (depending on how hot your oven is) to crisp up the skin. You will need to turn the tin every 5 minutes or so to achieve even crispiness all over.

Take the pork out of the oven and leave to rest for 20 minutes.

Tear the meat on a large board, roughly chop the crackling and scatter over the top. Sprinkle with the coriander (cilantro) and spring onions (scallions). You can either dip the pork into the dressing or spoon it over.

Crispy, Sticky Chicken & Vinegar Slaw

One of my biggest joys of life is eating in restaurants (even, at times, on my own). I love researching restaurants, deciding where to go, and oftentimes, I'll go through the menu before I even get there (I am really quite geeky when it comes to these things). I love the rituals of a restaurant: the interaction with the front-of-house staff, starting off a meal with a glass of bubbly, and, ideally, watching the action unfold in an open kitchen. I also love fried chicken.

I developed this recipe during the Covid 19 lockdown because I could have none of those things. Takeaway just wasn't going to do. I wanted to invest some time. Set the table and, for the love of restaurants, eat with your hands.

Gochujang is a Korean spicy fermented chilli paste and is available to buy in some larger supermarkets and in Asian supermarkets.

Serves 4

8 free-range chicken thighs, boned
neutral oil, for deep frying
2 spring onions (scallions), finely sliced (optional)
1 small handful of coriander (cilantro), leaves picked (optional)
3–4 Tbsp crispy shallots (p.48, optional

For the glaze
2 Tbsp gochujang
1 Tbsp rice vinegar (or red, white, apple cider or moscatel)
2 Tbsp palm sugar or dark brown sugar
1 Tbsp soy sauce
1 garlic clove, finely grated
2½cm (1 in) ginger, finely grated

Cut each chicken thigh into 4, season with fine salt and leave in the fridge for 2–3 hours.

To make the glaze, combine the gochujang, vinegar, sugar, soy sauce and 1 Tbsp water in a pan. Place over a medium heat, melt together and simmer for 1–2 minutes. Take off the heat and add the garlic and ginger.

Blitz or whisk all the ingredients for the batter together, ensuring it's smooth and with no lumps.

Whisk together the vinegar, honey and oil for the slaw and pour over the vegetables and herbs in a large bowl. Season with salt and generously with freshly ground black pepper. Toss together until well coated.

If you are using a deep fat fryer, then heat to 180°C/350°F. Otherwise, fill a large heavy based pan halfway up with neutral oil and place on a medium–high heat. If you don't have a temperature probe to check if the oil is hot enough, drop a little piece of bread into the oil. If the bread sizzles and begins to brown within 30 seconds, then it's ready.

Prepare a tray with a rack, ready to drain the cooked chicken. Dust the chicken pieces in a little flour and then into the batter and coat well. In batches, so the pan isn't overcrowded, carefully drop the battered chicken (away from you) into the hot

For the batter

2 egg whites

150ml (5fl oz) buttermilk or soured (sour) cream

2 Tbsp vodka (gin or white rum work as well)

120g (4¼oz) plain (all-purpose) flour, plus extra for dusting

2 tsp fine salt

For the slaw

2 Tbsp vinegar (red, white, apple cider or moscatel)

1 Tbsp honey

90ml (3fl oz) oil (olive, rapeseed/ canola or sunflower)

4 big handfuls of finely sliced vegetables such as cabbage, red onion or spring onion (scallions), carrot, kohlrabi or peppers (bell peppers)

1 big handful of coriander (cilantro) and mint, leaves chopped

oil. Cook for 2–3 minutes on each side or until golden brown and crisp. Take the chicken out onto the prepared tray and cook the next batch.

Once all the chicken is cooked, place into a large bowl along with the glaze and mix together using a large spoon.

Pile up the chicken on a serving platter and top with spring onions (scallions), coriander (cilantro) and crispy shallots, if using. Serve alongside the slaw.

Ideas & Inspirations

+ Add nuts, or dried or fresh fruits to the slaw.

+ Obviously, a pile of chips (fries) or roast spuds of some description will go down a treat here.

+ A couple of years ago my partner's mum, Hetty, was halfway through cooking a meal when she had to pop out. She asked me to finish cooking the meal (it won't surprise you that this often happens to me, at my own mum's house, too).

She had covered a piece of salmon with store-bought mango chutney. I was a bit weirded out but it ended up tasting magical. Buy a good-quality mango chutney and smear it all over the cooked chicken and it will work with this slaw, too.

+ You can bake the chicken in a pan or oven, without the batter or the deep frying.

Winter Fattoush & Tamarind-Glazed Short Rib

This dish is a real feast of contrast. If you have time, cook the ribs low and slow on a barbecue for an extra level of smoky flavour.

I first made this dish for Cook for Syria, to raise funds for Unicef, back in 2016. It is by no means a traditional fattoush, and I encourage you to go out and try the real thing if you get the chance (or prepare the original at home).

Serves 4

4–5 Tbsp sumac dressing (p.81)

3–4 Tbsp parsley oil (p.55)

4–5 Tbsp tamarind glaze (p.40)

100g (3½oz) croutons (p.46)

4 beef short ribs

4 Tbsp unsalted butter

2 pears, cut in half, core removed

80g (2¾oz) cavolo nero, stalks removed and the leaves torn into pieces

extra-virgin olive oil

½ cucumber, cut in half lengthwise and seeds removed, thinly sliced

8 breakfast radishes, finely sliced and placed into iced water

4 spring onions (scallions), sliced

¼ head radicchio, roughly chopped

8 leaves yellow chicory (endive), roughly chopped

1 small handful of flat-leaf parsley, leaves picked

4 Tbsp mint, leaves picked

sea salt flakes (kosher salt)

4 Tbsp thick yoghurt

4 Tbsp pistachios, toasted and chopped

Heat the oven to 190°C/170°C fan/375°F/gas mark 5. Prepare the sumac dressing (page 81), parsley oil (page 55), tamarind glaze (page 40) and croutons (page 46).

Season the short ribs with fine salt, place into a roasting tin and into the oven for 3–4 hours or until the meat is falling away from the bone. Pick the meat off the bone into large chunks, once cool enough to handle.

Heat a large frying pan (skillet) over a medium heat, add the tamarind glaze and short rib pieces along with 2 Tbsp of the butter. Cook until all of the meat is coated in the glossy glaze. Keep warm.

Put the remaining 2 Tbsp of the butter into a large, ovenproof frying pan, gently melt and add in the pears, cut-side down, and brown for 1 minute. Place into the oven for 10 minutes or until golden brown and cooked through. Allow to cool. Cut into large chunks.

Bring a large pan of water to the boil with a little fine salt. Add in the cavolo nero and boil for 3–4 minutes or until tender. Drain, and allow to cool slightly before dressing with a little salt and olive oil while still warm.

To assemble the salad, in a large bowl, mix together the cucumber, cavolo nero, radishes, spring onions (scallions), radicchio, chicory (endive), herbs, croutons and pears. Season with sea salt flakes (kosher salt) and sumac dressing, to your liking.

To serve, spoon a dollop of yoghurt on the plate and place a pile of salad to one side. Scatter over some pieces of short rib, drizzle around the parsley oil and sprinkle the pistachios over the top.

Ideas & Inspirations

+ Make as many of the elements or as little of the elements as you want. You could leave out the meat or pears or parsley oil, for example.

+ This dish is suited for the colder months, but you could easily swap out things like the bitter leaves, pears and cavolo nero for ingredients to suit the season you are in.

ROOTS & TUBERS

Celeriac, Mandarin & Sunflower Seeds

Celeriac (celery root) is not the best-looking vegetable around but it is incredibly hardworking. This recipe is an adaptation of how they cook celeriac in Turkey, with lots of olive oil, onion, and a whole citrus fruit chopped up. On occasion they will also use quince. The acidity of the citrus really lifts the inherent earthiness of the celeriac.

You could also use tangerines, satsumas or oranges for this recipe. The purée provides great contrast, and really makes this a simple but very rewarding recipe.

Serves 4 V

6–8 Tbsp celeriac (celery root)
   purée (p.52)
100ml (3½fl oz) extra-virgin olive
   oil, plus extra to dress the salad
3 shallots, finely sliced
1 celeriac (celery root), diced
2 mandarins, diced with the skin on
2 big handfuls of bitter leaves
   such as chicory (endive)
   and radicchio
1 big handful of coriander (cilantro),
   leaves picked
vinegar (red, white, apple cider
   or moscatel)
4 Tbsp sunflower seeds, toasted

Prepare the celeriac (celery root) purée as on page 52. Keep warm.

In a large pan with a tight-fitting lid, add the olive oil and place over a medium heat. Add the shallots and celeriac and season with a little fine salt. Cover with the lid and gently cook, stirring every 5 minutes, for 10–20 minutes. Add the mandarins and continue to cook for 15 minutes or until everything is soft and cooked through. Allow to cool to room temperature.

Divide the purée across the plates. Combine the celeriac mix with the bitter leaves and coriander (cilantro), season with salt and dress with olive oil and vinegar, to taste. Pile up over the purée and scatter with sunflower seeds.

Ideas & Inspirations

+ Have the celeriac (celery root) and mandarin mix with a piece of steamed or roasted fish. To push the boat out a bit more, steam open some mussels (follow the method on page 143) and then take around 80ml (2½fl oz) of the cooking liquor from the mussels and whisk in cold butter to make a great sauce. Finish with chopped chives.

Potato Salad & Variations

Let's talk potatoes. Everyone has their favourite spud, and it is a vegetable of great importance in many countries around the world. This humble tuber carries a heavy history on its soil-stained shoulders, from its Incan roots, through to its (forced) colonial migration across the world, to its demise in the 19th century (with the Great Irish Famine to follow).

Potatoes are a bit of a point of pride in the Cypriot community. Cyprus potatoes are a prized island crop, and I probably would have to agree with those that proclaim them as the best (or one of the best) potatoes your money can buy. It is the red soil they grow in, true island soil, that gives them their rich and buttery flavour (this red soil is transported from the centre of the island to the coast just to grow these potatoes).

A potato salad is oh-so simple, and if you select your ingredients carefully and treat them with respect, it is the perfect way of showing off the much-loved potato. I am usually in the mood for a creamy version (doused in mayonnaise) or the green Cypriot version (as I call it), which contains an abundance of herbs (with mint taking centre stage), spring onion (scallion) and lettuce, and is dressed with copious amounts of extra-virgin olive oil and lemon juice.

Both versions require a good waxy potato (the Cyprus potato, of course, being the preferred type), cooked gently in salted water with their skins on until just tender. They should be soft but not falling apart. Drain them and leave them to cool just enough so you can handle them without burning your hands (warning: you may still feel a bit of a sting) and cut into small chunks.

For the **creamy version** I season the potatoes and dress in olive oil and vinegar while still warm, as when you add a dressing to something warm it tends to drink it up. Then, add your choice of creaminess, a good mayonnaise (p.75), soured (sour) cream, crème fraîche or thick yoghurt. A combination of mayonnaise and one of the latter acidic trio can be rather good, too.

You can also just use store-bought mayonnaise (I have some in my fridge at all times, at the behest of my mayonnaise-addicted partner); but, having said that, when the dish is as simple as a potato salad a homemade mayonnaise will go that extra mile on flavour. These creamy potatoes are fabulous by themselves, but you can add extra flavour with mustard, gherkins, capers, crispy bacon or herbs. The one thing I always add is an onion element – chives, spring onions (scallions) or just a chopped onion of some sort – because raw onion, potato and acid is a flavour trifecta I'm absolutely in love with.

For the **Cypriot version** I just dress the potatoes in a little olive oil and salt after cutting them into chunks. Adding the lemon at this point, while they are still warm, completely changes the flavour profile and means the lemon juice loses its vibrancy. Add the lemon juice and more olive oil while mixing in all your greenery at the end.

My final thought on these classic potato salads is about the stirring. For me I like to stir both versions once dressed, enough so that some of the potatoes start to break up a little and provide an extra contrast in texture.

Use these basic recipes and experiment with flavour combinations from the book, or create your own.

My Suggestions:

+ Add a good hit of Kyseri spice mix (p.56) into some mayonnaise (p.75) and coat the potatoes. Dust more spice mix over the top, along with some chopped chives.

+ Dice some cured beef or lamb fat (p.60) and crisp in the oven until golden. Drain the crispy bits on paper towel and keep warm. While the liquid fat is still hot, take 1 Tbsp and add some vinegar and a little splash of olive oil. Coat the potatoes in this and add some chopped tarragon, season well with sea salt flakes (kosher salt) and serve with black garlic purée (p.51). Finish by sprinkling over the crispy fat.

+ Toss the potatoes through one of these dressings: za'atar (p.85), charred onion (p.234) or miso and lemon (p.84)

+ Dress warm diced potatoes with a little olive oil, vinegar and salt. Once cool, stir through egg borani (p.206) and chopped coriander (cilantro).

+ Coat the potatoes in a generous helping of chermoula (p.233), or mix the chermoula into some mayonnaise and then dress the potatoes.

+ While the potatoes are still warm, season with salt and dress with olive oil and vinegar. Once cool, coat in garlic yoghurt (p.157) and chopped parsley. Serve with chilli sauce (p.157).

+ Cut thin slices of a garlic sausage (chorizo, merguez or sujuk) and crisp up in their own oil in a frying pan (skillet). Take off the heat, add a little olive oil and vinegar of choice. Take some warm boiled small potatoes with their skin on (new potatoes, Jersey Royals, Ratte or Charlotte) and gently crush and add to the pan. Season well with sea salt flakes (kosher salt), add in some fresh herbs and spring onion (scallion) and serve warm.

228

Potato & Black Olive Güveç

A güveç is an earthenware clay dish used for slow-cooking dishes in Turkish cuisine – a Turkish casserole dish, so to speak, but I absolutely hate the word casserole and I think it does no justice at all to the finger-licking deliciousness of a dish tended to with love and care for so many hours.

A güveç will usually contain some kind of diced meat or fish with vegetables, some potatoes and a liquor made from water and sun-dried pepper paste. Like all stews and c*sseroles, a güveç will need rigorous seasoning and strong flavours to make it work.

Serves 4 VG

100ml (3½fl oz) extra-virgin olive oil
4 garlic cloves, finely chopped
1 tsp fennel seeds, toasted
   and ground
250g (9oz) Turkish mild pepper
   paste (tatli biber salçasi)
2 Tbsp vinegar (red, white,
   apple cider or moscatel)
5 long, mild Turkish green peppers,
   alternatively use 2 green (bell)
   peppers, seeds removed,
   finely sliced
2 spring onions (scallions), sliced
   into 1cm (½in) rounds
80g (2¾oz) good-quality black
   olives, pitted, roughly chopped
500g (1lb 2oz) waxy potatoes
   such as Cyprus, Desiree or
   Charlotte
1 handful of flat-leaf parsley,
   finely shredded

Heat the oven to 200°C/180°C fan/400°F/gas mark 6.

Place the oil and garlic into a pan over a medium heat. Sizzle until the garlic starts to turn golden brown. Immediately add in the ground fennel and pepper paste and stir thoroughly, cooking for a few minutes. Add in the vinegar and take off the heat. Add the sliced peppers, spring onions (scallions) and olives.

If you are using Cyprus potatoes, I would recommend peeling these, otherwise leave the skins on and slice the potatoes lengthwise into 1cm (½in) slices. If using big potatoes, cut 1cm (½in) slices widthwise. Coat the potatoes in the pepper mix and tip into a roasting tin. Sprinkle over a little fine salt.

Place into the oven and roast for 35–45 minutes or until the potatoes are soft and the top is all dark and gnarly. Top with parsley and serve.

Ideas & Inspirations

+ This would be a great side to a roasted chicken or some steamed fish. Or keep it veggie and pair with a simple salad, something like gem, dates, crispy lavash & feta (p.106).

Chermoula Beets, Dates & Pistachios

Until the tender age of about 32, beetroots (beets) and I did not get along. My mind was changed after a visit to Coombeshead Farm, chef Tom Adam's Cornwall outpost where he quietly lets his food do the talking while he is off chasing his hand-reared Mangalitsa pigs through the forest. Beetroots grown by a neighbouring farm were served as part of a first course at a dinner that went straight to the top of my list of favourite meals that year (and the next too, incidentally). They were the sweetest, earthiest beetroots I had ever had, with a texture approaching that of fudge. Like any true foodie geek, I ambushed Tom after dinner for tips and tricks. His dish inspired me to give beetroots another go.

Chermoula is a North African condiment and works really well with the flavour of beetroot. If ever I form an all-girl punk band, I think I will call ourselves the Chermoula Beets.

Serves 4 VG

800g–1kg (1¾–2¼lb) beetroot (beets) – a selection of different colours, if you can find them

5 Medjool dates, pips removed and chopped into 6

25g (1oz) pistachios, toasted and chopped (p.49)

For the chermoula

1 small handful of flat-leaf parsley, finely chopped

1 small handful of coriander (cilantro), finely chopped

¼ red onion, finely chopped

½ chilli, finely chopped

¼–½ lemon, juiced

1 small garlic clove, finely grated

½ Tbsp vinegar (red, white, apple cider or moscatel), plus extra for the beets

50ml (1¾fl oz) extra-virgin olive oil, plus extra for the beets

½ tsp smoked paprika

Heat the oven to 200°C/180°C fan/400°F/gas mark 6.

Wrap the beetroot (beets) in a foil envelope and place on a baking sheet. Place into the oven and cook for 45–90 minutes, depending on the size of the beetroot, until a skewer or tip of a knife inserted into the beetroot comes out easily. Leave to cool slightly. Using a small knife, peel the beetroot and then cut into random-shaped chunks.

Turn the oven down to 140°C/120°C fan/275°F/gas mark 1. Coat the beetroot in a little olive oil and salt and scatter across another lined baking sheet. Place in the oven and cook for a further 2–3 hours or until the beetroot have shrivelled a little, a bit like a sun-blushed tomato.

Remove from the oven and, once cool, coat in a little olive oil, vinegar and salt.

To make the chermoula, combine all the ingredients and season to taste. Alternatively, you could blitz all the ingredients in a food processor into a rough paste.

Spoon the beetroot across a serving plate and top with the chermoula. Scatter over the dates and pistachios.

Carrots, Charred Onion, Basil & Pumpkin Seeds

These glazed carrots are the same ones I use in the carrot borani (p.238), which is, I admit, quite a complex dish. I came up with this simpler dish when I was planning on putting the borani back on the menu at the restaurant but realized that most of the chefs on my service at that time were relatively new to the cooking game. They were part of 'Selin's Army', recruited by my head chef Laurence and I at a time of great need at the restaurant (and when professional chefs were few and far between). I sent out a social media post asking for anyone who had ever had the desire to try their hand at working in a professional kitchen to get in touch. My only requirement was that they work hard and have

passion. I ended up with a really lovely bunch of people who would come in now and then and lend us a hand – students, artists, lawyers – some of whom ended up changing careers and joining the ranks of professional chefs permanently. These glazed carrots were right up their alley.

If you are lighting the barbecue, these carrots will very much enjoy hanging out on the grill for a while once they've been glazed. The onion dressing also works well as a condiment, especially mixed through some mayonnaise.

Serves 4 V

1L (35fl oz) vegetable glaze (p.39)
2–3 Tbsp basil oil (p.55)
4 carrots, peeled
4 heaped Tbsp thick yoghurt
2 Tbsp pumpkin seeds, toasted
(p.49)

For the charred onion dressing
2 onions
2 Tbsp vinegar (red, white,
apple cider or moscatel)
5 Tbsp extra-virgin olive oil

Prepare the vegetable glaze (page 39) and basil oil (page 55).

Place the vegetable glaze in a wide-based pan and gently bring to a simmer. Add the carrots, season with fine salt and cook on a gentle heat for 6 minutes. Turn the carrots over and repeat. To check if a carrot is cooked, insert a skewer or tip of a small knife into the thickest part of the carrot – you should be able to remove the skewer/knife fairly easily. I like to serve the carrots just cooked, but if you prefer them softer, then cook a little longer. During the cooking process, if the glaze reduces too much, then top it up with a little water. Remove the carrots from the glaze and set aside. The glaze should be thick and syrup-like – if it isn't, reduce a little further.

For the dressing, place a griddle pan over a high heat. Cut the onions into quarters, place them into the pan and leave for 3–4 minutes, each side – you are looking to blacken them on either side. Alternatively, you could cook the onions under a preheated grill.

Place the onions into a small blender along with the vinegar and olive oil. Blitz to a coarse purée. Season with fine salt, to taste. Check if you're happy with the amount of acid, too.

As a final flourish, I like to char the carrots in a hot griddle pan or on a barbecue, but this is completely optional.

Cut the carrots into irregular shapes and toss with a little bit of the glaze.

Spread some yoghurt across the bottom of a plate, scatter the carrots and pumpkin seeds on top, add a drizzle of basil oil and dot around the charred onion dressing.

Parsnips, Cavolo Nero, Ricotta & Tomato Yuzu Jam

Hopefully, by this point I have gained your trust. This may sound like a really odd combination, but I am going to ask you to bear with me here. It is absolutely delicious and also a simple way of showing you (and you, in turn, others) that as long as you have acid, texture, contrast (and a little common sense), there is no limit to the dishes you can create.

Serves 4 V

4 Tbsp tomato yuzu jam (p.73)
4 parsnips, scrubbed clean
extra-virgin olive oil
4 slices of bread
1 garlic clove, halved
4 heaped Tbsp ricotta
15g (½oz) unsalted butter
8 chives, finely sliced

For the cavolo nero
3 Tbsp extra-virgin olive oil
2 banana shallots, finely sliced
35g (1¼oz) unsalted butter
2 garlic cloves, finely sliced
1–2 chillies, finely sliced with seeds
500g (1lb 2oz) cavolo nero,
   roughly sliced
175ml (5¾fl oz) white wine

Heat the oven to 220°C/200°C fan/425°F/gas mark 7 and prepare the tomato yuzu jam as on page 73.

Cut the parsnips into rough 2cm (¾in) pieces and toss in a bowl with a little olive oil and fine salt. Lay the parsnips out in one even layer on a lined baking sheet. Roast in the oven for 20–30 minutes or until they are soft and a little golden. Allow the parsnips to cool a little, then crush them using a fork or masher.

In a lidded pan large enough to hold the cavolo nero add the olive oil and place over a medium heat. Add the shallots and cook for 10 minutes, using the lid to create a little steam in the pan. Remove the lid, add the butter, garlic and chilli and cook for another 3 minutes. Add the cavolo nero and wine and season with fine salt. Bring up to the boil, place the lid back on and turn the heat down to its lowest setting. Cook for 15–20 minutes or until the cavolo nero has softened and is tender. Cook for another 5 minutes with the lid off to reduce some of the liquid.

Toast the slices of bread until crisp, allow to cool a little, then rub on either side with the cut garlic clove.

Warm through the parsnips, add the butter and the chives and check for seasoning.

Place the slices of toast on the plate and drizzle with olive oil, then spread the ricotta over the toast. Roughly spread over the parsnips, followed by 1 Tbsp of jam for each slice. Top with the cavolo nero and a final drizzle of olive oil.

Ideas & Inspirations

+ The cavolo nero itself is a perfect side, especially with the likes of roasted chicken, slow-roasted pork, pies, and steamed or roasted white fish, so be sure to give that a go. It's even great tossed through pasta.

+ You could replace the ricotta with pan-fried halloumi or a soft cheese. It's a special brunch or lunch idea for the weekend.

Carrot Borani, Cheese Shards & Muhammara

This recipe is complicated and I questioned including it in the book, but I decided that every dinner table should be graced by a vegetable-led dish that will blow everyone away. No doubt, this is that dish.

As there are a lot of elements to this recipe, you may wish to split up the work over a few days and then just reheat to serve at the temperatures recommended. If you are a barbecue enthusiast, you could smoke the aubergines (eggplants) over wood for an extra dimension of flavour.

Serves 4 V

3–4 Tbsp honey and shallot dressing (p.82)
4 Tbsp muhammara (p.69)
12–16 salt and pepper walnuts (p.43)
1 L (35 fl oz) vegetable glaze (p.39)
4 large leafy carrots, peeled; reserve 16 sprigs of carrot tops, soaked in iced water for 10 minutes
2 chicory (endive), red, white or both, leaves separated
1 radicchio, leaves separated
2 carrots, ideally different colours, peeled and thinly sliced
10 chives, finely sliced
sea salt flakes (kosher salt)

For the carrot borani
500 g (1 lb 2 oz) carrots, peeled and grated
extra-virgin olive oil, for frying
1 garlic clove, finely grated
45 g (1¾ oz) golden sultanas
190 g (6¾ oz) thick yoghurt

Prepare the honey and shallot dressing (page 82), the muhammara (page 69), the salt and pepper walnuts (page 43) and the vegetable glaze (page 39).

To make the carrot borani, place a large pan over a high heat. Add the carrots with a splash of olive oil and pinch of fine salt and cook, stirring regularly, for 8–10 minutes or until they are soft but left with a little bite. They shouldn't take on any colour. Once almost cooked, move the carrots to one side of the pan, pour in a drizzle more olive oil and add the garlic. Cook for 1 minute, then take off the heat. Add the sultanas immediately and stir. Leave to cool and, once at room temperature, stir in the yoghurt and season to taste.

Bring the vegetable glaze up to the boil and add the 4 whole carrots. Turn the heat down to a gentle simmer. Cook on one side for 5–7 minutes, then turn over and repeat. The carrots should be just soft enough that when you insert a skewer or tip of a knife it comes out easily, and the glaze should be syrup-like and golden. If the glaze is too sticky before the carrots are cooked, add a splash of water, or if the glaze doesn't look syrupy enough, remove the carrots and reduce further. Keep warm.

Optional step: I like to char the carrots over a smoky fire or in a hot griddle pan, cut into pieces and place back into the glaze.

Heat the oven to 180°C/160°C fan/350°F/gas mark 4. Place the aubergines (eggplants) on a baking sheet and roast in the oven for 45 minutes–1 hour or until they are very soft (keep the oven on for the cheese shards). Once they're cool enough to handle, cut them in half and scrape out the flesh.

238

For the aubergine purée

3 aubergines (eggplants), pricked
with the tip of a knife
90ml (3fl oz) double (heavy) cream
2 Tbsp extra-virgin olive oil
1 Tbsp caster (superfine) sugar

For the cheese shards

30g (1¼oz) unsalted butter, melted
4 sheets filo (phyllo) pastry
30g (1¼oz) tulum cheese,
crumbled
1 Tbsp nigella seeds, crushed
finely (optional)

Chop roughly and place into a sieve to drain any excess moisture. Place into a pan with the other purée ingredients and some fine salt. Gently bring up to the boil, then immediately take off the heat and pour into a high-speed blender. Blitz to as fine a purée as you can, adjust the seasoning to taste. Keep warm.

Line a large baking sheet, big enough to allow the filo (phyllo) sheets to sit completely flat, with baking paper. Brush the paper with a little of the melted butter and lay a filo sheet on top. Brush more butter on top. Take one-third of the cheese and distribute across the filo evenly in one thin layer, followed by a third of the nigella seeds, if using. Lay another sheet of filo on top, pressing down firmly. Brush the top with butter. Add another third of cheese and nigella across the filo, again in an even layer. Place another layer of filo on top and brush with butter. Sprinkle with the remaining cheese and nigella evenly and place the final layer of filo on top with a final brush of butter.

Place another sheet of baking paper on top and an identical baking sheet on top of that. Push down firmly. Remove the baking sheet and cut filo sandwiches through the paper into whichever shapes you like. (I like to cut rectangles.) Put the baking sheet back on top, then place into the oven and bake for 15 minutes, checking halfway through. The shards should be golden brown and crisp. Take out of the oven, remove the top tray and baking paper and allow them to completely cool.

Place the chicory (endive) and radicchio into a bowl along with the walnuts, thinly sliced carrots and chives. Season with sea salt flakes (kosher salt) and coat with the honey dressing.

To serve, spread a Tbsp of muhammara on one side of the plates using the back of a spoon. Place the salad leaves on top. In the centre, place a glazed carrot. Between 2 cheese shards smear enough carrot borani so it is roughly 1cm (½in) thick. Place the cheese sandwich to the right of the carrot. Finish with a dollop of aubergine purée and 3–4 carrot top fronds.

Ideas & Inspirations

+ Tulum is a Turkish crumbly cheese. If you can't find it in Middle Eastern supermarkets, you could use a hard cheese such as parmesan, finely grated.

+ The borani itself would make a great sharing dip, or you could sandwich it between the cheese shards for a very impressive canapé.

+ The muhammara and aubergine purée would make delicious bruschetta. Finish with crumbled cheese and herbs over the top.

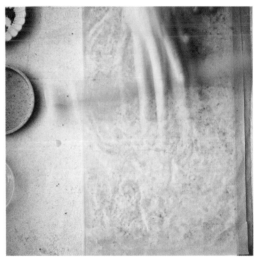

Glazed Jerusalem Artichokes & Za'atar

This recipe beautifully contrasts hot and cold. Jerusalem artichokes are underused by home cooks, although they are a frequent guest in restaurant kitchens. Their slightly knobbly and underwhelming outward appearance hides a wealth of flavour possibilities.

Serves 4 V

1L (35fl oz) vegetable glaze (p.39)

12–16 pieces crispy lavash (p.47)

6–8 Tbsp caramelized Jerusalem artichoke purée (p.52)

4–5 Tbsp za'atar dressing (p.85)

500g (1lb 2oz) Jerusalem artichokes, cut in half

8 Medjool dates, pips removed and cut into 6

extra-virgin olive oil

1 small radicchio, cut into random chunks

1 big handful of coriander (cilantro), leaves picked

1½ Tbsp lilliput capers, rinsed and roughly chopped

sea salt flakes (kosher salt)

4 pinches of za'atar

Heat the oven to 180°C/160°C fan/350°F/gas mark 4 and prepare the vegetable glaze (page 39), the crispy lavash (page 47), the caramelized Jerusalem artichoke purée (page 52) and the za'atar dressing (page 85).

In a large, ovenproof pan, bring the vegetable glaze up to the boil and turn off the heat. Add in the Jerusalem artichoke halves, cut-side down, and season with fine salt. Cover the pan with foil or a lid and place into the oven for 30–40 minutes or until the artichokes are cooked through and soft. Remove the artichokes from the pan and set aside. Reduce the glaze down to a syrup and add the artichokes back in. Keep warm.

Optional step: I like to char the artichokes over a smoky fire or in a hot griddle plan and place back into the glaze.

Place the dates into a large bowl and drizzle over a little olive oil. Use your hands to separate the dates that have stuck together. Add the radicchio, crispy lavash, coriander (cilantro), capers and warm artichokes along with a little of the glaze. Spoon over the za'atar dressing and season with sea salt flakes (kosher salt). Using your hands, coat everything with the dressing and then taste – if you feel the salad needs more dressing, then add more.

To serve, place a spoonful of the artichoke purée to one side of the plate and place a big handful of salad next to the purée. Sprinkle the plate with za'atar and serve.

Ideas & Inspirations

+ You can replace the dates in this recipe with a variety of dried fruits; some of my favourites are dried cherries or natural dried apricots.

+ The artichokes themselves make a great side dish with many different dishes but I love them with roasted scallops or steak. Scatter over some crispy beef fat (p.60) and you're onto a winner.

Celeriac, Lemongrass Caramel, Dried Shrimp & Citrus Peel Sambal

This is a lovely way to use the entire vegetable. Celeriac (celery root) makes great steaks but the trim and aromatics infused into the coconut milk and blitzed down also creates a wonderful sauce. In this recipe, I have combined Asian flavours with butter. I find that the richness of the butter works well to round out the flavours of Southeast Asian aromatics and, in this particular recipe, that sits beautifully alongside the celeriac.

Serves 4

4–5 Tbsp lemongrass caramel (p.65)

4 Tbsp dried shrimp and citrus peel sambal (p.66)

2 Tbsp basil oil (p.55, optional)

1 large or 2 small celeriac (celery root)

60g (2¼oz) unsalted butter

neutral oil, for frying

2 spring onions (scallions), finely sliced

1 Tbsp coriander (cilantro) stalks, finely sliced

For the sauce

1 x 400ml (14fl oz) can full-fat coconut milk

5cm (2in) reserved lemongrass trim, bruised and roughly sliced

3½cm (1½in) ginger, sliced

1 star anise

1 chilli, split in half

1 tsp fish sauce

1 lime, juiced

Heat the oven to 190°C/170°C fan/375°F/gas mark 5 and prepare the lemongrass caramel (page 65), the dried shrimp and citrus peel sambal (page 66) and the basil oil (page 55), if using.

Peel the celeriac (celery root) using a knife – you will need to trim approximately 3mm (1/8in) to remove all the gnarly skin. Cut the celeriac in half and then cut 4 semi-circle steaks around 2cm (¾in) wide (see page 246).

Cut the trim from the celeriac into small pieces and place in a pan along with the coconut milk, lemongrass trim, ginger, star anise and chilli. Place over a medium heat, bring up to a simmer, then turn down the heat to low and cook for 10–15 minutes or until the celeriac is cooked through and very soft. Remove the lemongrass, ginger, star anise and chilli and discard. Place the celeriac and infused milk into a blender and blitz to a smooth consistency. Pour the sauce back into the pan and season with a little salt, the fish sauce and the lime juice. Keep warm.

Melt the butter in a small pan over a medium heat and cook for 5–7 minutes or until the butter turns a deep golden colour. Take off the heat and leave the butter to cool a little before pouring through a sieve lined with paper towels to remove the sediment. Keep warm.

(continued overleaf...)

Heat a large, ovenproof frying pan (skillet) over a medium–high heat and add 2 Tbsp of neutral oil – if you don't have a pan big enough to hold all 4 steaks, then use 2 pans. Place the celeriac in the pan(s) and cook for 2–3 minutes or until golden brown. Season with a little fine salt, flip over, season again, and cook the same on the other side. Place the pan into the oven and cook the celeriac for 10 minutes, flipping them over halfway through. Insert a skewer (or the tip of a small knife) to check if they are cooked and the skewer can be removed easily.

To serve, pool some of the sauce into a bowl and place a celeriac steak in the centre. Spoon the lemongrass caramel over the steak to completely cover it. Spoon a few piles of sambal over the celeriac steak followed by a spoon of the brown butter. Top with the spring onions (scallions) and coriander (cilantro) stalks. Drizzle the basil oil around the sauce, if using.

Ideas & Inspirations

+ Instead of the sambal, try it with the cashew nut condiment (p.63).

+ Flaked smoked mackerel over the top of the celeriac steak works really nicely.

Potato, Cheddar Custard, Black Truffle & Egg Yolk

This is one for your dinner party table. It would work as an indulgent starter, followed by a slightly lighter main course, like the winter fattoush and tamarind-glazed short rib (page 222), for example, with its juicy crunchiness and high levels of acidity from lemon, tamarind and sumac.

Considering the wow-factor, it really isn't that difficult at all. Fresh truffle and truffle paste are quite pricey – you could consider scrapping them and just using a truffle butter or oil in the potatoes, or a truffle cheese in the custard to achieve that truffle flavour, instead.

Serves 4 V

100ml (3½fl oz) extra-virgin olive oil

1kg (2lb 4oz) Desiree potatoes
(you could also use Cyprus or Charlotte; keep the skin on for Charlotte), peeled and chopped into 1cm (½in) dice

2 bay leaves, torn

2 onions, finely diced

vinegar (red, white, apple cider or moscatel)

1–2 Tbsp truffle paste

4 egg yolks

sea salt flakes (kosher salt)

1 fresh black truffle

10 chives, finely sliced

For the custard

125g (4½oz) unsalted butter

60g (2¼oz) plain (all-purpose) flour

500ml (17fl oz) whole milk

200g (7oz) cheddar, grated
(I like Montgomery's)

3 egg yolks

Add the olive oil to a large, lidded pan and place over a medium–high heat. Add the potatoes, bay leaves and onions and season well with fine salt. Place a lid on top, turn the heat down to its lowest setting and cook for 30–40 minutes, stirring every 5 minutes to ensure everything cooks evenly and hasn't stuck to the bottom of the pan. The potatoes and onions should be cooking with no colour, and as they start to soften, the potatoes will break down, providing creaminess to the mix. If you feel the mix is cooking too slowly or too fast, then adjust the heat accordingly. Once cooked, adjust the seasoning with salt and freshly ground black pepper. Add the vinegar and truffle paste, to taste, and remove the bay leaves. Keep warm.

To make the custard, melt the butter over a medium-low heat and whisk in the flour to make a roux. Keep whisking the roux for 2 minutes to cook out the raw flour flavour. Add half the milk and whisk until smooth, then add the remaining milk. Season with fine salt and bring to a gentle boil, then turn the heat down to its lowest setting and cook, whisking every 5 minutes, for 20 minutes. Take off the heat, whisk in the cheese immediately to melt through. Beat in the egg yolks and adjust the seasoning, to taste.

To serve, place a pile of potatoes in the centre of a bowl and with the back of a spoon make a well in the centre of the mound. Drop an egg yolk into the well and season with sea salt flakes (kosher salt). Spoon the hot cheese custard all over the potatoes and egg yolk. Finally, grate over plenty of black truffle and sprinkle with the chives.

Miso-Glazed Chicken Fat Roots, Tahini & Shiitake Toast

This dish says 'I love you' like no other. There are a few steps to it and it takes a bit of time, but it will be worth every single second once you put it down in front of someone special.

I honestly think that the chicken skin is non-negotiable: chicken fat and miso on otherwise quite plain roots – who wouldn't want that?

Serves 4

3–4 Tbsp miso butter (p.70)

500g (1lb 2oz) chicken skin, roughly chopped (ask your butcher for chicken skin)

800g (1lb 12oz) root vegetables such as beetroots (beets), carrots, celeriac (celery root), onions, parsnip, shallots, swede (rutabaga) and turnips

8 small waxy potatoes such as Charlotte, Ratte or new potatoes

neutral oil, for frying

200g (7oz) shiitake mushrooms, finely chopped

2 banana shallots, finely chopped

2 Tbsp molasses such as date, grape or mulberry

2 Tbsp vinegar (rice, red, white, apple cider or sherry)

4 Tbsp black or regular tahini

4 slices brioche, cut 2cm (¾in) thick

15 chives, finely sliced

Heat the oven to 170°C/150°C fan/325°F/gas mark 3 and prepare the miso butter as on page 70.

Place a large, ovenproof frying pan (skillet) over a medium heat. Add in the chicken skin and season with fine salt. Once it starts to sizzle and fry, place the pan in the oven and cook, stirring occasionally, for 45 minutes–1 hour or until all the skin is golden brown and crispy, and the fat has rendered out. Remove the skin from the hot fat and place into a sieve to drain off.

Prepare the vegetables by peeling and cutting your selection into small, even sized 2–3cm (1in) chunks. If there are any that can be left whole, such as small shallots, beets or potatoes, then do so or cut them in half.

Add the vegetables to the liquid chicken fat, season with a pinch of fine salt and top with enough water to just about cover the vegetables. Place the pan on the stove over a medium heat. Cook the vegetables for about 20–25 minutes, or until the vegetables are cooked through and the water has evaporated, stir every 5 minutes. Once cooked, leave the vegetables in the fat ready to reheat later.

Place another frying pan over a medium heat and add a splash of neutral oil. Add the shiitake and shallots and gently fry for 15–20 minutes or until they've taken on a little colour and are cooked. Add the molasses and vinegar to the pan and cook for 1 minute. Take off the heat, add the tahini and stir.

(continued on page 251...)

Toast the brioche to a deep golden-brown colour and leave to cool. If the chicken skin has gone cold, reheat in the oven for a few minutes.

Drain the vegetables from the chicken fat and place into a fresh pan with enough water to coat the bottom of the pan. Warm the vegetables over a medium heat and, once simmering, add 2–3 Tbsp of miso butter and swirl the pan to emulsify the butter and water. Once the vegetables are glossy and coated in the glaze, they are ready. If the sauce splits, add a little water, stir and heat through to bring it back together. If the sauce looks too loose, add more miso butter.

To serve, spoon the shiitake-tahini mix onto the slices of brioche. Pile up the vegetables on the toast and sprinkle over the chives. Top with as much crispy chicken skin as you desire.

Ideas & Inspirations

+ If you don't have any molasses, use a little palm or dark brown sugar.

+ If you don't have time or inclination to render the chicken skin, then you could always roast or boil the vegetables and just toss them through the miso butter glaze.

+ Use leftover chicken fat for roasting potatoes and making into a vinaigrette to spoon over fish.

+ The miso vegetables themselves would be great alongside steamed or roasted white fish.

Index

Acknowledgements

Writing a cookbook is certainly not a one-woman show. A whole crew of people are needed, from those physically putting the book together to those on the cheerleading squad. Every one of them is essential and I couldn't have done this without them.

Firstly, a huge thanks to everyone at Quadrille. You have managed to shape this book into exactly what my vision was, even though I couldn't quite explain it to you in words. In particular Sarah Lavelle for taking a leap of faith in me to write this. Stacey Cleworth for being a mastermind editor and coherently pulling together all of my scribbles. Claire Rochford and Luke Bird for being absolute magicians in creating the beautiful design of this book.

Zoe Ross from United Agents, for all your professional support and help, especially in getting the proposal together.

To all of my British and Dutch family, for your constant and unwavering support. It's very comforting to know you are always cheering me on.

Chris Terry, for the incredible photographs and all the giggles. You are such a pro; it was pure joy to work with you on this book. Anna Wilkins for sourcing all the props (you absolutely nailed it) and for always knowing exactly how the cutlery should sit.

Peter Gordon, you are forever an inspiration. You taught me to cook freely. The way I create recipes would not have been possible without your guidance. You're my hero.

Diana Henry, humbled to receive your very kind words. It means a lot for you to read and understand this book so intrinsically.

The teams at my restaurants past and present, thank you for doing all the hard work so I can create. I couldn't do this without you.

Laura Christie, my business partner extraordinaire, who always gives me the space to explore new ideas and new beginnings.

And, of course, to my one and only Steph. We made this book happen together, at a time when the world has never looked so uncertain. After the initial shock of lockdown waned, I decided to write this book in the ample time at home I finally found I had. It turns out trying to write a book in the scariest of times was not as easy as I thought. You never let me give up and you never lost faith that I could do it. I don't say this lightly, but I really couldn't have written this book without you. I can't thank you enough for your help and your endless read-throughs to make certain it was perfect. I'm in awe of your incredibly smart mind and generosity. I love you now and always.

Publishing Director Sarah Lavelle
Editor Stacey Cleworth
Head of Design Claire Rochford
Designer Luke Bird
Photographer Chris Terry
Food Stylist Assistant Stephanie de Goeijen
Prop Stylist Anna Wilkins
Head of Production Stephen Lang
Production Controller Katie Jarvis

Published in 2021 by Quadrille, an imprint
of Hardie Grant Publishing

Quadrille
52–54 Southwark Street
London, SE1 1UN
quadrille.com

Cataloguing in Publication Data: a catalogue record for this book is available
from the British Library.

Text © Selin Kiazim 2021
Photography © Chris Terry 2021
Design © Quadrille 2021

ISBN 9781787137288
Printed in China